TWAYNE'S WORLD AUTHORS SERIES

A Survey of the World's Literature

Sylvia E. Bowman, Indiana University

GENERAL EDITOR

SPAIN

Janet W. Díaz, University of North Carolina, Chapel Hill

EDITOR

Juan Rodríguez de la Cámara

TWAS 423

JUAN RODRÍGUEZ DE LA CÁMARA

By MARTIN S. GILDERMAN
Temple University

TWAYNE PUBLISHERS
A DIVISION OF G. K. HALL & CO., BOSTON

Library of Congress Cataloging in Publication Data

Gilderman, Martin S
  Juan Rodríguez de la Cámara.

  (Twayne's world authors series; TWAS 423)
  Bibliography: pp. 141–45
  Includes index.
  1. Rodríguez de la Cámara, Juan, 15th cent.
PQ6425.R8Z68   868   76–28774
ISBN 0–8057–6195–0

Contents

About the Author

Martin S. Gilderman received his Ph.D. in Spanish literature from the University of Missouri in 1968. He has taught at Ohio University (Athens), Rutgers, and Temple University, and has also served as an administrator at the latter. His publications have appeared in *Hispania, Revista de estudios hispánicos* (Alabama), *Actas del IV Congreso de la Asociación Internacional de Hispanistas,* and *Boletín de Filología Española* (Madrid). He has also published poetry in the *AAUP Bulletin* and *Haiku Highlights.*

In addition to his publications, he has given papers at the Northeast Modern Language Association in 1971, 1973, and 1974, and has served as secretary and chairperson, respectively, of that organization's Medieval Spanish Literature section. In 1971, he read a paper at the Fourth Annual Congress of the International Association of Hispanists (Asociación Internacional de Hispanistas) in Salamanca, Spain.

His interests are not solely limited to medieval Spanish, since he has also given papers on Puerto Rican literature and studies, most recently at Pennsylvania State University.

Preface

The year 1492 marked the beginning of what has come to be known as the *Siglo de Oro,* or the Golden Age in Spain—both in politics and in literature. Spain's vast political empire was matched by the brilliance of some of the greatest literary figures in history—Garcilaso de la Vega, Lope de Vega, Cervantes, Calderón de la Barca, and Quevedo. In 1492, the last phase of the reconquest had been accomplished by the surrender of Moorish Granada and the discovery of America occurred. The Inquisition had then been in operation for more than a decade. The era of civil wars ended in 1479, and in 1492 Ferdinand and Isabella became coequal sovereigns, with joint powers encompassing the entire Iberian Peninsula.

What seemed so solid in 1492 seemed completely chaotic only forty years earlier, both in politics and in literature. In 1452, King John II of Castile ruled by virtue of his favorite, Don Alvaro de Luna, and after a period of civil wars, the nobles succeeded in having the favorite beheaded, leaving the country divided in its loyalties between the monarchy and the upper nobility. In literature, the acceptance and integration of humanism—the literature of pre-Christian Rome and Greece—which was to be one of the great foundations of Spanish literary excellence in the Golden Age, was little more than an exotic import which had yet to take root and flourish. New literary genres and influences were appearing in Spain, but many were rejected.

On the social level, there were the burning questions of the rights of women and of Jews, and it may safely be said that the year 1492 marked a low point in the fortunes of both these groups. After the beginning of the Inquisition in 1481, Jews were forced either to convert or to suffer the consequences, and after the end of the fifteenth century, the equality of women ceased to be the burning issue it had been in years prior to the coming to power of the Hapsburgs.

During the first half of the fifteenth century, the best known authors were the Marqués de Santillana, Jorge Manrique, and Juan de Mena. The author we wish to present is little known outside of Spain, yet he is the creator of Spain's first sentimental novel, *Siervo libre de amor* (*The Emancipated Slave of Love*) and a number of very interesting poems and other prose works. For the modern reader, Juan Rodríguez will be significant for three reasons: as defender of the absolute equality of women, as champion of the cultural heritage of his native Galicia, and as constant critic of the social inequalities in the courtly love code. All of Juan Rodríguez's works reveal the social and political upheavals of his era, an era of transition in which commonplaces of medieval thinking were being severely criticized but wherein no new systems had yet come along to take their place.

It is the custom of literary critics to "rediscover" an author and point out his importance because he has a message for contemporary audiences. Juan Rodríguez is such a figure, and in the following pages I hope to demonstrate that the thoughts he expressed in his time are today relevant once more. As creator of a new literary form, the sentimental novel, Juan Rodríguez went beyond the confines of codified male and female roles to protest against the unhealthy atmosphere of the royal court and to present arguments for his own liberation. While doing so, he sought to remind his readers that his homeland, Galicia, was the true center of courtly love, and not Castile; as a result, he elevated Galicia to the status of a shrine. All of the ideas present in *The Emancipated Slave of Love* occur throughout his other works, and the troubled times they portray will at times appear familiar to readers more than a half a millenium removed in time.

It will also be our purpose to reevaluate and place in proper historical context the literary and social phenomenon known as courtly love. Rather than viewing courtly love as a single, unified set of rules governing the courting customs of men and women of the nobility, we shall attempt to show that courtly love was a dynamic process with origins in France, and when it spread to other areas of the world, such as Spain, it was changed radically.

We will show that courtly love, with its assumed superiority

Preface

of the lady, was challenged by Spanish writers in general and vigorously so by Juan Rodríguez, who declared himself the movement's leader by virtue of his life—his banishment from the Castilian court because of a supposed love affair with a woman of the upper nobility—and his works—his mastery of the form and content of courtly love literature.

All English translations herein of Juan Rodríguez's works, both prose and poetry, are my own. All of the prose works cited are taken from Antonio Paz y Melia's 1884 edition of Rodríguez's works published in Madrid. In addition, I have made no attempt to change or modernize the spelling. Poems not found in Paz y Melia's edition include the three chivalric ballads, "Ardan mis dulçes membranças" and "Planto de Pantasilea." I have similarly not chosen to indicate which manuscripts the poems are found in, since this would be of interest only to professionals and not to a broader public.

In conclusion, I wish to thank Professors Gerald Wade, Janet Díaz and Alberto Porqueras-Mayo for their helpful hints and their encouragement.

MARTIN S. GILDERMAN

Temple University, Philadelphia, Pennsylvania.

Chronology

1350–   Macías, the most famous of the troubadour martyrs for
1369   love, figures prominently in the contemporary literature.

1406–   The reign of king John II of Castile, who wrote poems
1454   and invited poets to his court.

1430   Juan Rodríguez arrives at Assisi in the company of Cardi-
        nal Juan de Cervantes and meets several key figures of
        the Italian humanist movement, such as Andreas Sylvius,
        the future Pius II, whose sentimental novel, *The History
        of Two Lovers* (*Historia de duobus amantibus*), may
        have influenced Juan Rodríguez's *The Emancipated Slave
        of Love.*

ca.   Current presumed date of composition of Juan Rod-
1438   ríguez's prose works, *The Emancipated Slave of Love,
        The Triumph of Women,* and *The Seat of Honor,* the
        latter two being dedicated to Queen María, wife of
        John II.

1442   Juan Rodríguez takes his final vows for the priesthood
        and is ordained in Jerusalem, thus permitting him to
        return to Spain.

ca   Juan Rodríguez dies at the convent which he founded at
1450   Erbón.

1884   First edition of his complete works published in Madrid.

CHAPTER 1

The Life and Times of Juan Rodríguez

I Life and Legend

VERY little is known in fact about the life of Juan Rodríguez today, yet the influence he exerted in his lifetime and for about a century after his death was considerable. His poetry was quoted by contemporaries in their own works, as was the custom of the era,[1] and his sentimental novel, *The Emancipated Slave of Love*, may have influenced other now more famous works, such as Diego de San Pedro's *Cárcel de amor* (*The Prison of Love*) and the novels of Juan de Flores.[2] Yet more importantly, his life, or more correctly perhaps, his legend, was a profoundly moving experience for writers of the fifteenth and sixteenth centuries. For the writers of that period, Juan Rodríguez was not just a poet and novelist; he was the lover of a woman of the highest nobility, and a man who claimed for himself the leadership of the courtly love movement and the right to interpret courtly love customs as he thought they applied to contemporary social mores. As we shall see in the next chapter, the term courtly love in the early fifteenth century implied a social code which defined the role of men and women in a feudal, hierarchical manner with the woman, by virtue of her superior social position at court, the bestower of favors upon a socially inferior male who was ever careful to remain in her good graces.

As far as actual facts are concerned, two of Juan Rodríguez's biographers[3] place the poet's birthdate at the very end of the fourteenth century and give as his birth site the diocese of Erbón in the area of the town of Padrón, located several miles outside of Santiago de Compostela, the world-famous shrine of St. James, patron saint of Spain, in Galicia. It is known that he was of the minor Galician nobility, since his family's coat

13

of arms, that of the house of Cámara, is described in a famous
treatise on nobility and heraldry.[4] In his early years, he served
at the court of John II of Castile, and during these same
years he became a page of the future Cardinal Juan de
Cervantes, which some critics have suggested signifies that he
was of the poorer class of nobles.[5] It is at this point that the
biographical picture becomes cloudy and the possibilities for
a legend emerge. Sometime during his stay at court, he fell in
love with a woman of prominence. The identity of this woman
has never been ascertained, mainly because Juan Rodríguez
took such pains to conceal it. Nevertheless, in a fashion typical
of troubadours since the days of the late eleventh century, his
poetry and prose contain veiled hints and frequent allusions
to a woman of *estado desigual* (unequal and therefore "higher
station"). Rumor and conjecture have sought to identify this
woman as one of the ladies-in-waiting to the queen, María of
Aragón, wife of John II, but the mysterious lady's identity
remains unknown. According to Juan Rodríguez's own account
in *The Emancipated Slave of Love*,[6] the indiscretion of a
trusted friend cost him his lady's favor, again a frequent oc-
currence in the literature of the troubadours. Whether or not
he was truly exiled from Spain after falling out of favor with
his lady as is suggested in one of his letters,[7] has likewise not
been determined.

Juan Rodríguez appears to have traveled extensively in the
service of Cardinal Cervantes. One of Juan Rodríguez's biog-
graphers, Father Atanasio López, has surmised that Juan Rodríguez's inspiration to enter the priesthood may have arisen
from his meeting with St. John of Capistrano, who was with
Cardinal Cervantes at Assisi in 1430.[8] In one of his poems,[9] Juan
Rodríguez mentions the city of Basle, Switzerland, site of a
famous Church Council which commenced in 1431, and at which
Cardinal Cervantes was a known participant. Because of the
Cardinal's illustrious contacts, Juan Rodríguez may well have
met some of the more prominent figures of the Italian Renaissance, such as the future Pope Pius II, Aeneas Sylvius, whose
sentimental novel in Latin, *The Story of Two Lovers* (*Historia
de duobus amantibus*), may have influenced Juan Rodríguez's
own *Siervo libre de amor* (*The Emancipated Slave of Love*).

It appears that Juan Rodríguez entered the Franciscan Order sometime in the 1430s,[10] and took his first vows to enter the priesthood in 1441 while still in Italy, with his final vows in 1442, after he had journeyed to Jerusalem. Finally, he left the Holy Land and returned to his native Galicia, where he apparently founded a convent at Erbón. Today, the convent still stands, but there is no trace of Juan Rodríguez anywhere. All that remains is a street in the town of Padrón which bears Juan Rodríguez's name.

Juan Rodríguez's journeys after leaving Spain are reflected in his works, for he visited what were for him the three holiest shrines in all christendom—Rome, Jerusalem, and Galicia—and these journeys are partially reflected in the third section of *The Emancipated Slave of Love*, "The Tale of Two Lovers."

There are two difficulties in establishing the truth about Juan Rodríguez's life: one is his constant attempt to equate his name and personality with that of his famous predecessor, Macías; the other is the confusion which was created in 1839 by the publication of an anonymous, fictionalized biography entitled *The Life of the Troubadour Juan Rodríguez (Vida del trovador Juan Rodríguez del Padrón)*.[11] This manuscript, which some believe was published in the late fifteenth or early sixteenth century, depicted Juan Rodríguez as an Arthurian figure whom two queens find irresistible. According to this apocryphal work, Juan Rodríguez was a native of Aragón who came to the court of the Castilian King Henry IV (successor to John II) and immediately attracted attention because of his great beauty, courtesy, and prowess in the lists. He awakened the interest of a mysterious lady who had him come to meet her in a dark cave, wherein she confessed her love, but refused to show her face or reveal her identity. After several such encounters, she finally showed him her face and promised to wear his flesh-colored garter in her hair on the next festival day. While observing the women of the court in the company of his friend in whom he had confided all his secrets, Juan Rodríguez suddenly noticed that it was the queen herself who was wearing his garter. His friend, unable to contain his surprise, shouted to him to take notice. The queen realizing then that her knight had told of their meetings to an outsider, became furious, although Juan Rodríguez took no notice at the time. Later, when they had their usual rendezvous, the queen vented her fury upon him and proclaimed him banished from Spain forever and demanded that he burn all the gifts which she had bestowed on him. With his heart heavy laden he did her bidding and burned all the queen's jewels, money, and tresses. Accompanied by his friend, he bade Spain farewell and headed immediately for the French court. Upon his arrival, the queen of France[12] instantly fell in love with him and took advantage of her husband's absence to honor him with her favors. On realizing that she was with child, she asked him to take leave of her and the court. After departing and traveling through France, he was set upon in a cowardly fashion and slain by a group of French knights.

The above fanciful tale, which was based partly on Juan Rodríguez's life and partly on events portrayed in the third section of *The Emancipated Slave of Love*, was considered authentic until Pedro José Pidal, who discovered and published the anonymous, apocryphal "biography," admitted that it was nothing but a fiction.[13]

Another major difficulty in establishing an authentic biography of Juan Rodríguez concerns his attempts to link his name with Macías, who prior to Juan Rodríguez, had been a legend in his time and for the generation which followed. Like Juan Rodríguez, he, too, was a Galician and a troubadour, a court poet in the service of a noble. Unlike Juan Rodríguez, however, Macías was not banished from Spain but rather, it has been the custom to believe, really did "die for love." It is generally agreed that Macías flourished in the reign of Peter the First of Castile, in the latter half of the fourteenth century, and was presumably a page in the household of one of the masters of Calatrava.[14] While serving at the master's household, he fell in love with a young maiden, in whose service he continued even after she was married. Because he did not desist from paying court to this lady, her jealous husband contrived to have him killed. As two versions of the legend have it, either he died in jail or he died of a wound inflicted by the jealous husband who thrust his lance at him.[15] However, such was the fame of Macías that he was known for centuries as the prototypical martyr for love, idealized not only in the works of Juan Rodríguez and other troubadours of the fifteenth century, including Juan de Mena and the Marqués de Santillana, but also by the great figures of the Spanish Golden Age—Lope de Vega, Góngora and Calderón de la Barca—and in the romantic era of the nineteenth century by Mariano José de Larra.

Because of Juan Rodríguez's conscious attempts to link his name with his more famous countryman's, the former's works should be understood in part as his desire to conceive of himself as a continuer of the tradition of martyrdom for love. Although he did not write in Galician,[16] but rather in Castilian, and although he did not actually die for love but was merely banished, nevertheless there are elements in his works which are unequivocally Galician; while the allusions to Macías himself are clearly intended to link the two so as to recall such knightly figures as Lancelot and Galahad. Juan Rodríguez, however, is clearly the superior author and his works survive on their merits alone, whereas those of Macías are mediocre at best.[17]

II *Literary Significance*

Despite the fame he achieved in his lifetime for his work as a poet, Juan Rodríguez's major contribution to Spanish literature is prose, *The Emancipated Slave of Love*, Spain's first sentimental novel. Previous to Juan Rodríguez, love had been treated in three ways in medieval literature: as earthly, sensual love, with no thought of spirituality, as in the Ovidian tradition; as spiritual love, with no hint of sensuality, such as love of God; and, finally, as the code of courtly love, in which the lady, by virtue of her superior social position, became the *belle dame sans merci*, and the knight a slave to her caprices. *The Emancipated Slave of Love* incorporates all three of these traditions but transcends them to attain a view of love more in keeping with modern thought: love as a relationship between two equals.

As the sentimental novel later developed, it became noted for impossible love, tragic death, cruel parents, and rebellious offspring willing to die for love. The original contribution of Juan Rodríguez was to create a genre glorifying *both* and to view love as a rebellious act culminating in death. *The Emancipated Slave of Love* was merely the beginning of a long series of works in Spanish literature which were openly critical of courtly love either because its ideals were impossible or because it placed men in a subservient position. By the time Cervantes wrote *Don Quijote,* courtly love was totally unacceptable to the generality of Spanish culture, something practiced only by madmen. The Spanish genius had developed a sense of male-female equality and *The Emancipated Slave of Love* went far in reasserting this equality against a code which held both men and women in a kind of bondage.

III *Premessianic Spain*

Two literary historians of enormous prestige, María Rosa Lida de Malkiel, and Américo Castro, have respectively termed the first half of the fifteenth century in Spain the pre-Renaissance[18] and the preimperial age,[19] and both appear to be correct. As medieval modes of thought such as Scholasticism, and art forms such as allegory, were being questioned or severely modified, the new imports from Italy—humanism, Neoplatonism and the classical genres—had barely arrived and had only just begun to make an impact. In terms of politics, the first half of the fifteenth century saw a regency[20] and then a weak monarch, John II, ruled mostly by his favorite, Alvaro de Luna,[21] who sought to enhance the prestige of the monarchy by crushing the nobles, although this ambition ultimately failed and ended with the beheading of the favorite at Valladolid in 1452 after an uninterrupted series of civil wars.

Johan Huizinga termed the era "The Waning of the Middle Ages."[22] Although he was careful to point out that the phrase applied only to France and the Low Countries, Huizinga's term has some relevance to Spain, for he felt that the great display and pageantry of the era served to disguise the fact that the institutions of feudalism and chivalry were slowly dying, and only pompous, empty spectacle kept them propped up for a period of two centuries. Seconding him in this idea was Raymond L. Kilgour,[23] who traced the decadence of the nobles in France mainly to the House of Burgundy, scoring the ineffectiveness of chivalry, that is, cavalry, mounted warriors clad in armor, against the English during the Hundred Years War. Because of the rise of the kings of France with their efficient standing armies of foot soldiers, the institution of chivalry quickly proved inoperative.

Despite the similarities of Spain's condition to that of France and the rest of the continent, there were enormous differences. In Spain the institutions of chivalry and feudalism, which did not take hold in the same way nor as firmly, did not suffer as radical a decline. The nobility in the first fifty years of the fifteenth century were overwhelmingly still warriors and not courtiers. They were needed to fight the Moors in the south (Granada), the Portuguese in the west, and to secure the Aragonese Empire in the Mediterranean. To this may be added their constant struggles to retain their lands and privileges against the encroachments of the monarchy. Two factors did, however, pose a threat to their existence. Throughout Europe, the monarchy had sought to lessen the influence and power of the traditional, landed nobility by creating a new nobility based on services performed for the crown, services other than military. Thus we read of newly created nobles given coats of arms, privileges at court, and even parcels of land. And in Spain, the members of the new nobility were occasionally converted Jews who, fearful of attacks by the peasantry,[24] or of the jealousy of the old nobility, sought refuge in the crown, and often attempted to add to the power of the throne at the expense of the nobles.

One of the most serious consequences of the social upheaval of the fifteenth century was the new role of women and converted Jews.[25] The latter, because of their affluence and skills, became trusted counselors of the monarchy, and their presence, felt everywhere in commerce, finance, scholarship, and the arts, made them the object of attack—physical by the peasantry and intellectual by the Church and the Catholic artists. The presence of influential women at court, such as Queen María, wife of John II, enhanced the position of women everywhere, but also made them the object of attack once they too achieved a degree of prominence as the result of the praise of their admirers. The Torrellista controversy unleashed a streak of misogynism which polarized the artistic community and ultimately dealt courtly love a death blow when, in the succeeding centuries, great authors such as Fernando de Rojas,[26] and even Cervantes, saw fit only to ridicule it.[27]

The early fifteenth century produced a strange series of ironies, for the weak king, John II, sought to augment the prestige of the Castilian court by inviting poets from all parts of the realm to ply their art, and he himself set the example by composing verse.[28] At this particular juncture, there were poets from the upper nobility, like the Marqués de Santillana, lower nobility, like Juan Rodríguez, and even converted Jews like Juan Alfonso de Baena. Scholarship and literature, which were previously considered fit only for clerics and Jews, were now being practiced by the nobles also, even though many of them did so purely out of economic necessity.

The era which saw a flourishing of poetry was also the era of great philosophic and theological crises which had begun in the thirteenth and fourteenth centuries and were as yet unresolved. The great Thomistic synthesis of faith and reason had been undermined by such thinkers as Duns Scotus and William of Ockham, and the Italian school of Neoplatonism, which had come to Spain in the time of John II was, previous to the era of the Catholic Kings, imperfectly assimilated. Concurrently, the Church was undergoing the most serious internal threat of all—the Great Schism—which would not be healed until the period which we are studying was over. The literature of this period was profoundly influenced by the divorce between faith and reason,[29] and it is truly ironic that when courtly love did arrive in Castile, it was modified by the new philosophy of nominalism and the events which created popes in both Rome and Avignon.

Another great irony is that despite the skepticism in religion and the continuous civil wars, Spain was in an expansionist posture. Her energies had not yet been greatly reduced by the union of Castile and Aragon and the conquest of Granada, and she was striking out in various directions. Her ambassadors had penetrated to Central and Eastern Europe, she took possession of the Canary Islands, and frequent jousts and tourneys took her knights to all parts of Europe. As her navy began to prepare itself, we read of the heroic exploits of Count Pero Niño[30] and his battles against the English and Moorish pirates, as well as his epic jousting in France. The era of the early fifteenth century produced many heroes, but it had not as yet produced *the* hero or heroes.

It is difficult not to believe that Américo Castro is correct in his statement that Christian Spain in the early fifteenth century not only was in a preimperial era, but also in a premessianic era. The rule of the Catholic kings, Ferdinand and Isabel, galvanized Spain and launched the Empire. Before them, however, many "messiahs" were sought and some even declared themselves as such. One such figure, misunderstood by many, is Juan Rodríguez de la Cámara: misunderstood in part because he claimed to be a messiah, *the* messiah of courtly love.

CHAPTER 2

Courtly Love Poetry

I The Origins of Courtly Love

W HAT we call courtly love poetry in the late fourteenth and early fifteenth centuries in Castile began in the late eleventh and early twelfth centuries in the south of France. The origins of the vogue remain obscure because several influences were present concurrently, and each may have played a part in forming the complex patterns of thought which culminated in the formation of *Fin'Amors*, the "true" or "refined" love of the troubadours.[1] There are generally three influences cited: 1) the May Day rites and other pre-Christian folk customs; 2) neo-Latin poetry in dialogue known as the *invitatio amicae* ("invitation to a friend"), written by wandering clerics; and 3) Hispano-Arabic love songs, based on chivalric and Neoplatonic themes, sung by slave girls purchased or captured by Christian knights during their journeys into Spain or even the south of France itself.[2] During the May Day rites known as *calendas maias* ("the beginning of May"), young women were free to choose their partners and go with them into the forest to dance and sing, and a queen was chosen from among the married women to preside over the festivities; she had the power to refuse her husband and accept other lovers on that day.[3] In contrast, little can be said about the neo-Latin verses of the wandering clerics, but it is felt that these poems evinced a new sensibility on the part of the Christian men toward women and revealed that the educated class, at least, had begun to find virtue in the opposite sex. Most influential of all, for modern scholars, is the influence of Hispano-Arabic Neoplatonism and verse forms. All of the themes present in the poetry of the Provençal troubadours are found in the works of the Arabs of Spain in the two centuries preceding the Golden Age of Provençal literature.

Two of the most recent and significant revaluations of courtly love studies have been by Moshé Lazar and René Nelli. Lazar's approach, which may be called "philological," has attempted to clear up the confusion surrounding courtly love terminology.[4] As Lazar explains, the term "courtly love" is an expression whose meaning has varied through time. Thus, "courtly love" at the time of the Provençal troubadours of the late eleventh and twelfth centuries is distinct from "courtly love" of the thirteenth, fourteenth, and fifteenth centuries in France and elsewhere.

Lazar maintains that expressions such as *fin' amors*, ("subtle love"), *verai' amors*, ("true love"), and *amor bona*, ("good love"), which the Provençal poets used to describe the highest form of love between a man and a woman, have been misunderstood by generations of medievalists, who have sought to equate these terms with Ovid, Neoplatonism, Marian worship, or any kind of love in which physical fulfillment is either not present or of secondary significance. For Lazar, the Provençal poets may have spoken of spiritual delights, but they never lost sight of their primary goals—a kiss, an embrace, the contemplation of the lady's naked body, and, ultimately, *del surplus* ("the rest").

Misunderstandings have arisen because love, as spoken of by the Provençal troubadours, could not be reconciled with either Ovidian practicality, Neoplatonic purity or the medieval Christian dichotomy of the spirit and the flesh. Lazar claims that for one short period in the history of medieval literature, the late eleventh and twelfth centuries in the south of France, the lyric poetry of the troubadours depicted a society in which an adulterous relationship between men and women of the aristocracy was totally amoral; that is, if the rules of *fin' amors* were maintained, not only was there spiritual uplift in the process of self-denial, but, ultimately, and indeed of necessity, physical satisfaction.

Conjecturing about the possible origins of the amorality and spiritual fulfillment of *fin' amors*, Lazar claims that the social milieu of the south of France produced a new class of landless, errant aristocracy, who traveled from court to court seeking the protection of the more powerful barons. At the same time, the clergy of the region was known for its moral laxness in comparison with the clergy of the north. In addition, there was much contact between southern France and Arabic Spain at this time, with Lazar noting that southern France may have even been closer to Spain culturally than to northern France.

A further element in his arguments is that one of the strongest concepts in Provençal poetry of the twelfth century is that of *jovens* (imperfectly translatable as "youth"), which may have derived from a synthesis of the Arabic *futuwwa*, which meant "generosity," "liberality," and "moral purity," and *fatà*, meaning "generosity" and "comradeship." Together, the two terms may have combined to mean a brotherhood of persons possessing the qualities of generosity and moral purity which are associated with "youth," although not necessarily with those young chronologically.

Lazar points out that concepts traditionally associated with courtly love, such as suffering for love, "dying for love," sadness when separated from the beloved, are often not any more important than the lover's impatience with suffering and his delight in the sensual pleasures of self-denial, but only up to a point. Equally important is the troubadour's insistence upon aristocratic codes of behavior, which bespeak good breeding, and his fear of rivals—other troubadours who may sing more loudly or more sweetly the praises of his lady. For these reasons, the troubadour was very much a political animal, who, while thoroughly in love with a woman of greater wealth and power than himself, was also aware of the need to maintain his position against all rivals and to keep his lady's identity secret, although this may not have been as important as some scholars have presumed, since many husbands were not that concerned about the attentions of a mere troubadour.

Another of the myths exploded by Lazar is that of the importance of *mezura* ("temperance," "self-control") in the lover's mode of behavior. The ideal may have been the balanced, courteous, pretender, but too often *mezura* was an impossible goal, and the irrational lover fallen into an intemperate state of *desmezura* was more often the case.

Lazar also distinguishes between "courtly love" and "courtesy" (*cortezia*). As he explains it, "In effect, one cannot be courteous, that is to say, have a noble and generous soul, if one does not love according to the code of love proposed by the troubadours."[5] *Fin' amors* is the source of all the virtues—temperance, youth, joy, courtesy, bravery, and valor, and "courtesy" is the natural result of the man who loves according to the code of *fin' amors*, *Cortezia*, for some troubadours, may have meant the sum total of all the courtly virtues of a perfect gentleman, and for others the highest form of morality to which the courtly lover could aspire.

Another approach, which may be called "ethnological" or "anthropological," is that of René Nelli. According to Nelli, the knights of southern France who went to the Crusades were not so much influenced by the Arabic culture of the Orient—Syria, that is,—as they were by that of Al-Andalus, Arabic Spain.[6] It was here during the tenth and eleventh centuries that Islamic authors extolled the praises of young, unmarried girls of the aristocracy, usually princesses, and spoke of dying for love. According to the Arabs, the act of loving was the sign of a noble and generous heart, and he who could keep himself chaste while ever remaining in love could eventually transcend love and attain spiritual perfection. Yet it was only through three stages—love of the maiden, which led to a love of virtue or the "divine forms" or ideas, which ultimately led to love of God—that a man could attain such perfection. While absent from his lady, the lover was plunged into profound misery and on the field of battle he would hope to die for her, for such a death would be sure to bring him salvation and, of course, total union in the afterlife.[7]

In the poetry of the Provençal troubadours, the concept of *Fin'Amors* is not identical with either of the three types of love mentioned above, but there were many similarities. For the troubadours, it was necessary to love a woman who was already married, for those unmarried were *to be married* and did not possess the necessary serenity of soul. Also, the woman was nearly always superior in social status to the lover and there were at least two good reasons for this: first, there was a strong current of misogynism in medieval Europe, and women were generally held to be inferior unless they were socially prominent; second, many of the lords of the manor were absent, fighting in the Crusades, either in the Orient or in Spain, and the lady of the manor became in effect the feudal lord or *midons* as the poets would often refer to her. Thus for the Provençal troubadours, courtly love was, among other things, a bridging of the social gap for the male, and a bridging of the spiritual gap for the female.[8] The historical factor is of great significance when discussing courtly love, for the recognition of woman's worth occurs at a time when women such as Eleanor of Aquitain[9] achieved great political power and thus became conspicuous; it was they whose favor had to be sought by a host of male admirers.

It has often been pointed out that *Fin'Amors* was unique in that there was nothing analogous to it either in antiquity, where the only kinds of love experiences were friendship and conjugal love at one extreme and lust at the other, or the Middle Ages, which did not recognize any other kind of love except conjugal love or the love of God. *Fin'Amors* should be regarded as a delicate balance between natural passion and purely spiritual love in which the woman ceases to be important *qua* woman and becomes merely a means toward a spiritual end which is, ultimately, contemplation of the Divine Essence.[10] In courtly love, the lover is ennobled *because of* rather than *in spite of* his physical love, and his lady never ceases to be a woman of flesh and blood. In essence, the lover is ennobled by his willingness to suffer for his lady and this signifies postponing the love act as long as possible if not forever. It is this very suffering which purifies or refines love, and he who can maintain himself the chastest is the greatest lover. If he or his lady cannot refrain and their love must be consummated, then they are both still worthy, although a distinction must then be made between "pure love" and "mixed love,"[11] but the latter is still *Fin'Amors*, even though it fails to reach absolute perfection.

Much of the difficulty in reading courtly love poetry derives from the fact that the one essential but unfortunate circumstance of courtly love was the need for secrecy. Should the identity of the lady become known, the poet was in danger of death or banishment. And there were penalties for the lady as well. Therefore, the poets had recourse to *trobar clus*, the "dark

rhyming," in which the lady's identity was couched in a kind
of code language which appeared in the last stanza or *tornada*.[12]

An unknown prose writer among the Provençals[13] codified the
lover's service as being divided into four parts: that of pretender (*fegnedor*), aspirant (*pregador*), accepted lover (*enten-
dedor*), and coequal (*drut*). The last term occasions many
problems, for the word *drut* had several meanings, the earliest
of which was pejorative:[14] namely, the poet's rival or member of
the upper nobility who was his lady's social equal or even superior, who was perhaps her physical lover, but not her "courtly"
lover, and was therefore spiritually unworthy of her. Slowly,
however, the term *drut* came to mean the highest degree that
the lover could attain. The other three steps of servitude involved a long apprenticeship, whereby the lover was chosen
by his lady, forced to serve her without hope of reward, until
at last he was permitted a small favor such as an embrace or
at most a kiss. At last, in the third stage, he was subject to the
ultimate test, the *asağ*, in which he had to prove his love and
restraint (which were one and the same) by lying next to the
lady, either fully clothed or nude, occasionally in the presence
of witnesses, and not yield to the temptations of the flesh.

Despite the difficulties for the modern reader in understanding such heroics, it must never be forgotten that the lover was
a social inferior who had to prove his worth (*pretz*) by his
service. His passion and his reason were always at war with
one another, but it was assumed that his reason, his noble nature,
would win out. If he was willing to undergo the rigors of passion, he would be rewarded by the joys of love, which were considered to be wholly spiritual in nature, even though there
were, of course, the kiss, the embrace, and other tangible factors.
As seen, the lady's identity had to be kept strictly secret at all
times, for there were slanderers (*lisongiers*) about who doubted
the motives of both parties and who often sought to trick the
lover and gain the lady for themselves.

One of the outstanding contributions to the subject has been
Nelli's differentiating between chivalric and courtly love.[15] According to Nelli, chivalric love was the love of the upper
nobility, who sought to win the lady by acts of courage and physical prowess. "Dying for love" in these terms meant dying in

battle, and there was no thought of restraint or chastity when it came to the "rewards" for service. The lover might be ennobled by his love for a beautiful woman, but chivalric lovers were of the high nobility to begin with and did not need to prove their worth by a long period of vassalage. Courtly love, on the other hand, was the love practiced in the court, the love of an inferior for a superior, a vassal for a suzerain. The lover could not win his lady by physical feats of arms; he could only win her by his virtue, devotion, and suffering. If a rival was of a superior caste or if there was a husband present, the lover had to allow the lady her physical lovemaking, knowing all the while that this was not "true" love (*Fin'Amors*). Thus the lover felt inferior and humiliated on the one hand and superior on the other. Socially and perhaps physically, he could never hope to equal his rivals; spiritually, however, he was convinced of his superiority.

Naturally, the Church did not sanction courtly love, even though it did tolerate it for more than a century. The difficulty was that the Church could not allow that a physical being, in this case, a woman, could produce anything resembling spiritual sensations, even though practitioners of courtly love never claimed, as did the Arabs of Spain, that love of woman could produce love of God. Because of the Church's stress on the duality of the flesh and the spirit and its insistence upon Aristotelian hierarchies which tended to relegate woman to an inferior status, any thoughts of woman's ennobling man or elevating him spiritually were out of the question. Therefore, at the end of the thirteenth century, courtly love was at last condemned by Étienne Tempier, the bishop of Paris.[16] However, this was really unnecessary, for by that time, courtly love had died a natural death. Before it was "exported" from France to the rest of Western Europe, poets had ceased to pay reverence to the lady as a woman of flesh and blood and had converted her into a spiritual entity or, even more radically, into the Virgin herself.[17] When courtly love came to Spain, it did not "take" in the Court of Castile until it had first passed through the Courts of Aragon-Catalonia and Galica-Portugal. By the time of Juan Rodríguez, too much had happened in Spain and Europe to allow it to reblossom in its pristine form. When the seed was sown in Castile, the new plant that emerged was scarcely recognizable in its new environment.

II *The Coming of Courtly Love Poetry to Castile*

The first lyric poetry in Castile was not written in Castilian, but rather in Galician, a dialect of Portuguese. During the mid-thirteenth century, King Alphonse X, "The Wise," composed Songs to the Virgin (*Cantigas a la Virgen*) in Galician, and in the latter part of the fourteenth century, love lyrics were being written in Galician by Castilians who wrote in a very castilianized Galician.[18] So deep was the influence of Galician upon Castilian that many of the earliest Castilian love lyrics contained quotes from Galician authors like Macías,[19] or Galician phrases and terminology translated literally.[20] The earliest poets, such as Alfonso Álvarez de Villasandino, were bilingual, as was the Marqués de Santillana. But when Castile effectively attained political hegemony over Portugal, the former also achieved a kind of literary hegemony, and many would-be poets traveled to the Castilian court of King John II rather than to Portugal or Santiago de Compostela.[21]

The traditions of Castilian verse did not accept either the verse forms or the emotional content of the Galician-Portuguese. Whereas the latter referred the parallelistic strophe (two- or three-line stanzas with a refrain, with each successive stanza repeating the first line of the previous stanza), the former preferred the *estribillo glosado* ("glossed refrain"), in which a short two- or three-line stanza was followed by an expansion of the thought contained in the original refrain, and then the refrain would be repeated.[22] Whereas the Galician-Portuguese were fond of indulging their emotions by personifying them as characters or dwelling on the memory of the absent lover, the Castilian mind preferred legalistic argumentation, relying on a heavy dose of casuistry and ecclesiastical parody.[23] When a Galician such as Juan Rodríguez found himself at the Castilian court, he wrote in Castilian (if he wrote any poetry in Galician, it has yet to be discovered), but there remained in his work much that was Galician. As a writer he sought to excel and outdo the Castilians at their own game, for he had been born into a courtly love tradition that had been practiced for two hundred years prior to its arrival in Castile. It is our view that he was an outsider upholding his own cultural identity by infusing the Castilian love lyric with exotic elements that bespoke the "country" of his origin. In addition, and what is perhaps most important of all, he lived the life of a troubadour, falling in love with a woman of the upper nobility and writing poetry in her honor. When he fell from favor and was banished, he visited the two holiest shrines in all of Christendom, Rome and Jerusalem, and then returned to what all Spaniards consider an equally holy shrine, his native Galicia, only to sing of love again, but this final time in prose.

III "Siete gozos de amor" ("The Seven Joys of Love")

As was mentioned above, the Castilian mind had a penchant for legalistic language which manifested itself in courtly love poetry in a number of ways, all of which tended to shed unfavorable light upon the love relationship. The two devices most frequently employed by poets of the fifteenth century were casuistry and ecclesiastical parody. The parodying of religious themes and applying them to aspects of courtly love may well be Spain's outstanding contribution to the field of amorous verse.[24] In "Siete gozos de amor," one of the lengthiest and most famous of Juan Rodríguez's poems, the poet takes as his theme the feudal contract inherent in the courtly love relationship; he claims to have served his lady well and therefore feels entitled to the rewards (*gozos*) for his labors, but he has yet to receive any. Thus he begins his lament with an invocation to the God of Love himself:

Ante las puertas del templo	Before the doors of the temple
do recibe 'l sacrificio	wherein love receives the sacrifice,
Amor, en cuyo seruicio	love, in whose service
noches y dias contemplo,	I contemplate night and day,
la tu caridad demando,	Your pity does beseech,
obedescido Señor,	o most revered master,
aqueste ciego amador,	this blind lover
el qual te dira cantando,	who will recite to you in lyric verse,
si del te mueue dolor,	if his pains do move you,
los siete gozos d' amor.	the seven joys of love.

The architecture of this poem, like that of the Gothic cathedral of the high Middle Ages, or the medieval scholastic treatise,[25] is quite complex in that it is divided into a prologue, seven main sections or *Gozos*, with each *Gozo* divided into three stanzas, and a finale or *Cabo*. The entire poem itself is a parody of the Joys of the Virgin as well as a further parody of the four stages of love which the lover must pass through in order to attain the status of coequal[26] who is rewarded by the lady's complete confidence and love.

The first *gozo* describes how the poet actually fell in love:[27]

El primer Gozo
El primer gozo se cante
causar la primera vista,
que la señora bien quista
comiença ser dell' amante,
quando a la ley verdadera
se muestra de bien amar,
le plaze de se tornar
ciego de hombre que era
ha creer y afirmar,
o mirir o defensar.

Yo solo diran que fue
el ciego contemplador
que cego tu resplandor
la ora que te mire.
El sol no pudo causar
con toda su claridad
lo que tu sola beldad;
mas no 's de marauillar;
¡si tanto o la meytad
fuesse la tu piadad!

De mouerte a compassion
no te deues retraer
ro ver bien y conocer,
aunque ciego, mi passion.
La pena del pensamiento
y deseo no complido,
aunqu' el sentido he perdido,
con doble sentido siento:

The First Joy
Let them sing that the First Joy
is caused by the first sight
of the lady when she of her lover
becomes beloved when,
according to the true law of love,
she deigns to show herself,
which causes her lover to turn blind,
and this I believe
and do affirm
or die, or else defend.

They shall say that I alone
was the blind worshipper
which your brilliance blinded
the moment I beheld you.
The sun could not cause
with all its clarity
what could your beauty alone
but one should not be surprised
if your pity
were as great or but a half.

Although my passion be blind,
I see well enough and know
that you should not
fear to show compassion.
The pain of my unfulfilled passion
and desire
I feel in a double sense,
even though I have lost all sense,

quanto mas mi muerte pido,   for the more
se dobla mas mi sentido.   I seek death,
                               the more my sense does yield.

According to Moshé Lazar,[28] the term "joy," (*joi*) as used by
the Provençal troubadours of the twelfth century, had no meta-
physical or Christian overtones. Originally, for such poets as
Bernard de Ventadorn, *joi* was synonymous with "erotic and
sensual enjoyment and not only sentimental exaltation."[29] *Joi*
might elevate a man's spirit, rejuvenate his body and his heart
(and William of Orange, the first of the troubadours, even went
so far as to declare that *joi* was the redemption of his flesh and
soul), but the essence of *joi* was physical, even though the
spiritual element was never lacking. In fact, it is only Bernard
de Ventadorn who sings of *joi* as "a sentiment intensely passionate, immoderate, irrational. In effect, joy which crowns love,
seizes man and transforms him irresistibly."[30]

The difficulties with the term multiply when *joi* is used as a
synonym for the lady herself, for all joy flows from her. Thus,
the temptation to equate the corporeal presence of a woman
with the Christian concept of *caritas* was irresistible for a poet
wishing to show his mettle in the manipulation of such a formi-
dable weapon as ecclesiastical parody. For Juan Rodríguez, with
a technique that can almost be described as "baroque," complains with many a flourish that he has been denied all of the
joys of love, and that as a result he dies a martyr; more specifically, *the* martyr of the courtly love movement.

Two further elements, however, serve to complicate the interpretation of the poem. First is the inability of the poet to accept
the usual conventions which, by his time, had become courtly
love dogma. Because the realities of his situation did not co-
incide with the formal conventions, the poet is obliged to lodge
a complaint, but he can do so only within the framework of a
complicated, legalistic argument which must first present the
love relationship as though it were a feudal contract, with
obligations on both sides, and then proceed to show that he had
fulfilled his part as vassal, but that the lady, his suzerain, had
not fulfilled hers. The element of ecclesiastical parody is deeply
intertwined with the feudal compact, for the poet, the faithful

believer in the religion of love, has kept his faith, but "joy," the synonym for *caritas,* or the lady's divine grace, has been denied him, and, therefore, such devotion can only bring salvation and the glory of martyrdom: the supreme martyrdom befitting the greatest of the courtly lovers since Macías.

The second complication is the folkloristic or Celtic element. As many Provençal poets routinely noted, it was the lady herself who initiated the love relationship, or, in the words of the troubadours, her beauty and virtue which caused her admirers to fall in love with her. This may only have been the result of the lady's superior social position which enabled her to take the lead; however, there is another interpretation. René Nelli has noted that in many cultures a woman was presumed to possess magic powers,[31] strange spells, and potions, even the magic power of beauty itself, which, by causing men to fall in love, gave women parity with man's superior physical strength. When the troubadours wrote, female beauty and whatever magic powers were present therein were considered good or benevolent, for they infused man with strength, both spiritual and physical, on the field of battle. Juan Rodríguez, however, interprets the spell of his lady's beauty as something powerful, attractive and yet malevolent; something which will lead him to his doom. This kind of female power, which is not present in either the Provençal or Castilian love lyrics, is present in neo-Celtic literature of the Middle Ages, in the ritual known as the *geiss,*[32] in which young women of the upper nobility arbitrarily chose men of inferior or equal social status and imposed impossible tasks upon them which would ultimately lead to their death. The reward for the male's service could of course only be in the afterlife.

Because of Juan Rodríguez's Celtic heritage, and because this same theme is exploited in his other works, there is every reason to believe that he is imputing this malevolent, fatalistic quality to his lady. Despite the more usual interpretation which might be given these three stanzas, it is our contention that Juan Rodríguez did not merely "fall in love," nor was he simply "plucked" from the multitude of his lady's admirers. But rather he is slowly, even legalistically, preparing for his eventual martyrdom which, according to the laws of the *geiss,* was inevitable.

In a more typical fashion, Castilian poets when complaining of the hardheartedness of their lady would contrast her with Christ or the Virgin in order to chastise her and beg that she show more compassion. Thus, in the second stanza, an allusion is made to the lady's beauty resembling the sun's, but this is nothing more than a case of ecclesiastical parody, for in the Middle Ages the sun symbolized Christ[33] who was infinitely compassionate, while his lady was not.

Also in a more conventional manner, the poet reveals the changes made in courtly love poetry as the result of Spain's particular historical situation. In the early fifteenth century, there was a great sense of military and religious fervor as the Christians were preparing to expel the Moors from their last stronghold, Granada. Thus we find a great concern for Christianity being referred to as the only "true faith," as contrasted with the Jewish and Islamic heresies. Thus, too, many "old Christians" were becoming concerned with the purity of their bloodlines. It is for this reason that Juan Rodríguez makes an allusion to the "true law of love" and himself as a true martyr for love in the same way that an "old Christian" of that time would allude to the "true faith" which was Christianity as opposed to the Semitic heterodoxy.

The very first favor that could be granted the lover, according to the Provençal troubadours, was the *bel semblans* or "fair countenance,"[34] and in the second stanza, the poet complains that he has yet to receive what is rightfully his:

El Segundo Gozo
El primer gozo fenesce
sin fenescer dessear:
el segundo es de cantar,
la contra del no fallesce.
El qual, segun la fe nuestra,
en que soy el mas costante,
es aquel primer semblante
que la señora demuestra
al sieruo adelante.

Solo yo, triste, dire,
deste plazer no gozando,

The Second Joy
The first joy ends
without wanting to end;
the second is to be sung,
the opposite of which does not end
Which, according to our faith,
in which I am the most devout,
is that first pleasant countenance
which the lady displays
to her servant thenceforth.

Only I, melancholy, shall say
of this pleasure (without enjoying it

que nuestra ley, mas amando
do lo que manda, passe.
Amador que tanto amasse
no digan que ser pudiesse;
yo solo diran que fuesse
aquel que la ley passasse
da amar y amor venciesse.

that by loving more than our law
demands, I transgressed.
Let it never be said that
there was ever a lover who loved
so much;
they shall say that I alone
was the one who overcame
the law of love and thereby conquered love.

En boz mas triste que leda
el segundo ya canté;
si del por ti no gozé,
por falta d' amor no queda.
El que ha d' auer victoria,
sin tu bondad ofender,
en amar, yo he de ser
de quantos posseen la gloria
o passar o fenescer.

In a voice more melancholy than
happy
I sang the second joy;
if I didn't partake of it
because of you,
it was not for lack of love.
He who will be victorious
in love without offending your virtue
shall be I of all who possess the glory
or die or pass away.

According to the language of love, the lady was often referred to as *midons* or "my lord," and the lover was her "serf" or "slave," for which reason Juan Rodríguez is quick to point out his abject status in the first stanza. However, he is also quick to point out that he is the most loyal or "constant," for loyalty was the foremost feudal virtue. In the second and third stanzas, he again lays the groundwork for his eventual martyrdom by insisting upon his heroism, for he and he alone "surpassed" the law of loving and thereby conquered love. That is to say that he was truer to the code of courtly love than to the lady herself and was willing to endure her hardheartedness.

In the third stanza, the poet resorts to the *trobar clus* or "dark rhyming" of the Provençal troubadours in which many words were double-entendres, especially words referring to the lady's identity or to the act of lovemaking.[35] Thus in the second half of the final stanza, *bondad* has a double meaning, referring not only to the lady's "kindness" and "virtue," but also to her "social position." *Gloria*, of course, is a loaded word which in his context signified the love act,[36] thus there is an implication of the lady's promiscuity.

Herein lies another basic difference between the attitude of the Provençal troubadours and the Spaniards. For the former, the lady was permitted by the poets to have her lovers as long as they were merely lovers in the physical sense. She was only promiscuous if she had more than one "courtly" lover.[37] Spanish morality, as is evident from the poetry of Juan Rodríguez and his contemporaries, could not countenance promiscuity on any level.

In the third *gozo,* there is a change of verse form, as we shift to the *coplas de pie quebrado,*[38] made famous by Jorge Manrique:

El Tercer Gozo
El tercer gozo es
el amante ser oydo,
recontando
los trabajos que despues
de su vista l' an venido,
desseando.
E! qual tiene por sentir
quien hasta aqui
el huego do suele arder
quiso a todos encobrir
y mas a ti,
por mas gloria merescer.

Si fue de mi ofendido
amor y sus servidores
algun dia,
fue por no ser entendido
qu' en biuo fuego de amores
yo ardia,
ni tu merced entendiesse
la tal flama
yo sentir y padescer,
con temor que no ardiesse
la tu fama
por causa de me valer.

Lo que el seso resistiendo,
tu ni otro pudo oir
jamas de mi,

The Third Joy
The third joy is
the lover's being heard
when he wishes
to tell of the cares
which, after seeing his beloved,
beset him.
This has he yet to feel,
he who until now
wished to conceal from all
the fire in which he burned,
and especially from you,
to attain more glory.

If love and his servants
were one day
offended by me,
it was because
they did not understand
that I burned
in the fires of love,
nor did your mercy recognize
the passion I feel and suffer
for fear that your reputation
might suffer
were you to recognize my worth.

What the mind resists
neither you nor anyone else
could ever hear from me

ya biua muerte muriendo,	who was already dying a fearful death,
con desseo de morir,	
te descobri;	for, desiring to die,
como 'l qu' es puesto a tormento,	I revealed your identity;
que por fuerça	like him who is put to torture and
su mal viene a confessar,	who, by force,
y tornando al sentimiento,	confesses his sin
mas s' esfuerza,	and then, returning to his senses,
de lo encobrir o negar.	tries all the harder
	to conceal or deny it.

In the second stage of love as described by the Provençal troubadours, the lover expected his lady to hear his complaints and his suffering. Here again Juan Rodríguez complains that this likewise has not been granted him and thus he has remained silent, and this silence should therefore merit him even greater "glory," in both senses of the word.

As has often been remarked, much of Provençal courtly love poetry is obscure in meaning because the poets were purposefully obscure, trying to allude to certain aspects of their relationship in vague terms or with a series of code words and double-entendres. The second and third stanzas of the above section are in this "dark rhyming" tradition. Both stanzas seem to be alluding to the supposed indiscretion which led to the poet's disfavor and his ultimate banishment. The second stanza apparently is referring to the fact that the poet was unable to communicate with the lady for fear that the lady's reputation would be in danger, since the affair was presumably adulterous and the parties involved of unequal social status. The use of the verb *valer* is significant, for it meant not only "to make worthy," but also "to recognize" or "to elevate in honor."

The third stanza seems to imply that because he could no longer contain himself, the poet indiscreetly revealed the relationship in a moment of weakness and thus committed the capital offense in the courtly love relationship, since secrecy was vital.

The fourth and fifth *gozos*, rather than describing a stage in the love relationship, deal instead with the lady's virtue and social position:

El Quarto Gozo

El canto va fenesciendo
del tercero,
mas no plañir y llorar;
menos caridad sintiendo
que primero,
del quarto vengo a tractar.
El qual es, pues que dezir
m' es forçado
donde 'l fuego concebi,
discreta señora serui
en estado
y virtud mayor de mi.[39]

El primer mouimiento
al segundo
nunca pudo contrastar,
auido conoscimiento
en el mundo
tu ser la mas singular.
Conozcan ser tu loança
mas deuida
las altas de gran poder,
pues la bien auenturança
d' esta vida
es virtudes posseer.

Como sea manifiesto
tu vencer
las virtudes en bondad,
por ventura desonesto
mi querer
juzgará tu voluntad;
mas porque veas el fin
desseado
de virtud no desuiar,
mi mote del seraphin
inflamado
te plega de blasonar.

El Quinto Gozo

El quarto gozo finando,
sin fin auer mis cuydados,

The Fourth Joy

The song of the third
is ending,
but not the weeping and the tears;
feeling less charitable
than before,
I shall treat the fourth;
which is, since I am
forced to say
wherefore I fell in love,
I served a discreet lady
whose virtue and social status
was superior to mine.

The first step
to the second
never could be stopped,
since it is known that
you are the most unique.
May the ladies
of the highest rank
recognize that your praise
is most deserved,
since the good fortune
of this life
is to possess virtue.

Since it is obvious
that you surpass
the virtues in worth,
perhaps your Will
might judge my love
illicit,
but so that you may see
the desired end of virtue
not go astray,
may it please you my motto,
"the inflamed seraphin"
to display.

The Fifth Joy

The fourth joy is ending,
without my cares dying,

mas siempre multiplicando, el quinto ya discordando, mis sentidos trabajados en sus males contemplando, es poder en la señora el seruidor entender su seruicio qualquier ora, ofresciendole plazer.	but always multiplying; The fifth joy, now disturbing my troubled senses contemplating their ills, is for the servant to know that his lady is aware of his service at any hour, affording him pleasure.
Pues mi seruicio no vees contrastar a las virtudes manifiestas que possees, ni demanda, segun crees, que tu buen desseo mudes, ni lo contrario dessees, no te sea cosa fuerte en grado lo recibir de quien piedad o muerte no cesa de te pedir.	Since you do not see my service in contrast with the obvious virtues you possess, nor does it demand, as you believe, that you vary your chaste desires, or that you seek virtue's opposite, may it not displease you to receive it from one who pity or death ceases not to implore you.
Si la tu gran discrecion, una virtud posseyendo, ya posee quantas son, · sin auer contracion, una sola fallesciendo, y las otras que tal son; para ser mas virtuosa gloria que tanto deseas, conviene que piadosa contra mí seas.	If your great discretion were to possess one virtue, already possessing all there are, without contradiction, were one to lack, what would be the value of the others? In order to be more virtuous, to attain the glory you so much desire, it is proper that you be forced to be piteous unto me.

These two *gozos* reveal the irony of Castilian courtly love poetry. By convention, the lady was always superior to her lover, either by true social position, as was usually the case, or was considered superior in virtue, if the poet himself was of the upper nobility.[40] For the poet, this meant that the more important the lady, the more significant he was, for all of his "worth" derived directly from her. If the poet was humble and accepted his lot, there were no problems, since the poet, as an inferior, was always grateful for any favors. If, however, the poet became in any way dissatisfied with the terms of the relationship, there would be constant complaining on his part and a sense of injustice. This was the case for many Castilian poets, who deemed it unmanly to subordinate themselves to a woman, no matter what her social status, and it was keenly felt and expressed by Juan Rodríguez. For that reason, references abound in "The Fourth Joy" to the lady's high position, since the poet wishes to boast that he is the lover of someone so important. He even ends with a motto or heraldic image of himself as the "inflamed (that is, passionate) seraphim," which, while offering the lady homage, also serves to show the intensity of his ardor which is always under control.[41]

But "The Fifth Joy," like "The First," employs casuistry in an attempt to move his lady to pity. In the second stanza, he argues that since his service has been honorable, she should at least grant him the rights inherent in the next stage of the courtly love process, which is to be her constant and trusted servant. However, the final stanza, which is a clever use of Scholastic argumentation, employs both casuistry and a double-entendre. Of the three theological virtues—faith, hope, and charity—the lady appears to be lacking in charity, and without this virtue, salvation or "glory," synonymous with the sex act, will not be hers. Thus the lady must be "charitable" in every sense of the word.

"The Sixth Joy" is the realization of the love act:

El Sesto Gozo	The Sixth Joy
Del quinto me despidiendo,	Bidding farewell to the fifth,
sin dar fin al triste canto,	without ceasing my sad song,
el sesto en boz de planto	to the sixth in a lamenting voice,
por orden vo prosiguiendo.	I proceed,
El qual es si la tardança	which is, if the delay
por ti cessa,	for you ceases,
de largo me ofrescer	to offer myself at last
la verdadera esperança	the true hope
o promessa	or promise
del deseado plazer.	of the sought after pleasure.
Quantos aman atendiendo,	They who love awaiting
desaman desesperando,	fall out of love despairing,

y yo menos esperando,	and I, when I least expected it,
mas en el fuego m' enciendo.	did more in the fires burn.
La voluntad no mouible,	The unmovable,
desseosa,	yet desirous will,
¿quien la puede constreñir?	who can restrain it?
Quando a Dios es imposible	When such a thing
la tal cosa,	is impossible for God,
yo no puedo resistir.	I cannot resist.
Esperança y desseo	Hope and desire
son en tan gran diuision,	are in such great division,
que segun la perfection	that because of
de la tu bondad, yo creo,	the perfection of your virtue,
aunque Dios te perdonasse,	I believe that even though
y la gente	God himself would pardon you,
no lo pudiesse creer,	and the people themselves
que tu merced no pecasse,	not believe it of you,
solamente	that your mercy would not sin,
por tu virtud mantener.	if only to keep your reputation intact.

As was usual in the courtly love relationship, the lover pleads for mercy, hoping that his lady will yield and grant him the *guerredon* or "reward" for his labors, but if she did yield, it could only be after the lover had proven his sincerity in the *asag* ritual mentioned above.[42] In this *gozo* the poet resorts again to casuistry in order to convince his lady to yield, assuming, apparently, that he has passed the test and is at the point of death unless he be quickly "rescued" by his lady's mercy. Using Scholastic reasoning, he maintains that God may grant man the gift of divine grace or *Caritas* (charity), but only the will is free to accept or reject it.[43] But if the will is not quickly touched by "grace" (that is, the consummation of love), it will soon be "lost" or "damned." In his concluding remarks, he returns once more to the premise that the lady will not yield simply because of her fear for her "virtue," to be understood as "reputation."

In the seventh and final *gozo*, we come to the final stage of courtly love, when the poet wishes to be regarded as the lady's coequal, or in the terminology of the anonymous codifier of Provençal courtly love, her *drut*:

El Seteno Gozo

Del sesto me delibrando,
sin poder mi gran firmeza
la sobra de tu crueza
vencer, mas acrescentando,
el final gozo nombrado,
solo fin de mis dolores,
es amar y ser amado
ell amante en ygual grado,
qu' es la gloria d' amadores.

Pues obra de caridad
es amar al enemigo,
conuiene que al amigo
ames de necesidad.
Si voluntad no consiente,
virtud la deue forçar
amar tu leal siruiente
en el grado trascendente
que t' ama sin mal pensar.

La muerte siento venir
del cuerpo no se que hagas;
mueuante las cinco plagas,
celos, amor y partir,
bien amar sin atender,
amar siendo desamado,
y desamar no poder,
pues no te pueden mouer
los gozos que te he cantado.

The Seventh Joy

Freeing myself from the sixth,
without my great constancy being
   capable
of overcoming your cruelty, which
   grows
ever stronger,
the final joy is named,
sole end of my woe,
which is for the lover
to love and be loved in an equal
   degree,
which is the glory of all lovers.

Since it is charity
to love your enemy,
it seems that you should love
your friend, of course.
And if the will does not consent,
virtue should force it to love
your loyal servant with the same
transcendent intensity that he loves
   you
without thinking ill of him.

I feel death coming;
I do not know what you will make
   of my body;
it died of the five wounds of love:
jealousy, being absent from one's
   lover,
loving well without waiting,
loving and not being loved in return,
and being unable not to love;
for the joys that I have sung to you
failed to move you.

Throughout "The Seven Joys of Love" the poet has sought equality or martyrdom, "equality" in the sense of being recognized as an equal, despite the social differences. In the second stanza of this *gozo*, he resorts to casuistry one final time in an effort to attain his goals, invoking the Christian duty of loving one's neighbor or, in this case, "friend," a frequent euphemism for "lover." And in the final stanza, there is again the use of ecclesiastical parody, as the lover compares his martyrdom to that of the crucified Christ, or, as one critic has held, St. Francis of Assisi.[44] Thus the five wounds become "the wounds of love," since all other measures have failed and this is his only "reward."

As was typical of the Provençal *cansos*, or poems of unrequited love, there is a *Cabo* or finale:

Cabo	Finale
Si te plaze que mis dias	If it please you
yo fenezca mal logrado	that I end my days
tan en breue,	so unfortunately and so briefly,
plegate que con Macías	may it also please you
ser meresca sepultado;	that with Macías
y decir deue	I be buried.
do la sepultura sea:	And wherever the sepulchre lies, it
Una tierra los crió,	should read:
una muerte los leuó,	"One land raised them,
una gloria los possea.	One death snatched them,
	May one glory take them."

In this final stanza, the poet's real intentions are laid bare: he wishes not merely martyrdom, but a linking of his name with that of his famous countryman's as one of the two great martyrs for love. Although Juan Rodríguez did not actually die for love as did Macías, the fame of his love affair and subsequent banishment was so great[45] that had any other poet written this stanza, it would not have meant so much.

IV *Conclusion*

"Siete gozos de amor" is Juan Rodríguez's most complex poem in that he uses every argument and device at his command to plead for recognition of his service to his lady. In so doing, he displays a typical Spanish male reaction against subservience in the courtly love relationship, even though in so doing he strikes at the basis of this relationship, that is, the elevation of woman to a spiritual level so high that men must go through a series of trials before they are deemed worthy to share her love as an equal. Despite his claims of humility and of being the

most loyal and the most constant of lovers, Juan Rodríguez, in a
fashion typical of his era, usurps the title of redeemer of the
courtly love movement by describing his own "passion" and his
own "prefiguration." Just as he was "doomed" or "prefigured"
to fall in love, suffer, and die of the "five wounds of love," so
was he "prefigured" to suffer the fate of his countryman, Macías,
the first martyr for love, who would assume the role of John
the Baptist in this strange "martyrology of love." In a parallel
fashion, Juan Rodríguez's fatal love affair and his attachment to
Macías are not only Christian but Celtic and nationalistic. He
describes his lady as having magic powers which seem to force
him to fall in love with her against his will, and which will
ultimately lead to his "death." Also Celtic in nature is his link
with Macías; this will reappear in a similar fashion in *Siervo
libre de amor* (*The Emancipated Slave of Love*), in which Juan
Rodríguez will actually establish himself as a direct descendant
of his countryman. It may be too much to say that Juan Rodríguez
conceived of himself as a reincarnation of Macías, a belief in
reincarnation being prevalent in Celtic countries;[46] but, if nothing else, the link is an assertion of the "country" of his origin,
Galicia, and perhaps even more important, his messianic claims
based on the fact that he is a noble and an old Christian, and
not a converted Jew.

The modern reader may have difficulty comprehending how
any realistic analysis of a love affair could be found in a poem
like "The Seven Joys of Love," in which the feudal rituals of
paying homage to the lady's superior social caste must be
acknowledged before any criticism of her actions can be lodged.
This can only be explained by an appreciation of the late Middle
Ages, when, as Huizinga correctly observed, formalities were
carried to extremes. Despite the almost "baroque" adherence to
form, which results in a poem bordering on being incompre-
hensible, "The Seven Joys of Love" affects the reader as a
brilliant *tour de force*, allowing the poet to vent his dissatisfaction with his lady by going to the absurd extreme of demanding
recognition from all around him—rivals as well as friends—as
first among martyrs. This, no doubt, was the highest social and
literary status to which someone like himself, who had fallen out
of his lady's favor, or "grace," could obtain.

CHAPTER 3

"The Ten Commandments of Love"

NO greater evidence can be found for the contention that
Juan Rodríguez considered himself the leader of the courtly
love movement than "The Ten Commandments of Love," another
lengthy ecclesiastic parody in which the God of love, in Jehovah-
like fashion, selects our poet as the bearer of the law to the
masses gone astray. In a manner similar to "The Seven Joys of
Love," in which the "joys" were ironic, for they were pleasures
or favors never felt or received, the so-called "commandments"
are also ironic, in that many of them stand in direct opposition
to the earlier precepts of the courtly love code.

As in "The Seven Joys of Love," the actual enumeration of
the commandments is preceded by an allegorical dream or vision:

La primera ora passada	When the first hour
de la noche tenebrosa,	of the shadowy night was past,
al tiempo que toda cosa	the time when all things
es segura y reposada,	are secure and rested,
en el ayre vi estar,	I saw in the heavens
cerca de las nubes puesto,	next to the clouds
un estrado bien compuesto,	a well-wrought throne
agradable de mirar.	handsome to behold.
En medio del qual vi luego	In the midst of which I then saw
ell Amor con dos espadas,	the God of love with two deadly,
mortales, emponçoñadas,	poisoned swords, all ablaze
ardiendo todas en fuego,	with fire,
para dar penas crueles	in order to inflict cruel pain
a vosotros los amantes,	upon you, o lovers,
porque no le soys costantes	because you are neither
seruidores, ni fieles.	constant servants, nor faithful.
De la terrible vision	Standing in great fear
estando con gran recelo,	of the terrible vision,

45

vna boz quebró del cielo
diziendo por este son:
¡O tu, verdadero amante,
bandera de mis batallas,
pierdese mi bien, y callas!
Hablarás de aqui adelante.

Diras a los mal reglados
amadores desleales,
a las penas infernales
que cedo seran juzgados
si no enmiendan su beuir,
la mi dicha ley guardando,
vicios, essores dexando
de los que suelen seguir.

La justa ley, amadores,
de que vos mando vsar,
y que os puede acrescentar
o menguar vuestros dolores,
si en partes mis mandamientos,
los quales voy prosiguiendo
segun que mas largo entiendo
declarar sin argumentos.

a voice broke from heaven
and spoke in this manner:
O you, true lover,
standard-bearer of my army,
all is being lost and you are silent.
You shall speak from now on.

You shall tell the ill-disciplined,
disloyal lovers
of the infernal pains
to which they shall be condemned
if they do not change their way of
    living
and observe my law,
leaving behind the wicked ways
they used to follow.

The just law, you lovers,
which I order you to obey,
and which can either augment
or diminish your suffering,
are my commandments,
which I shall intend to narrate
in accordance with my understanding
    at length
(and) without discussion.

In the history of amatory verse, the God of love has been depicted in a variety of ways, from Ovid's winged and purblind *puer Veneris* ("son of Venus") to Charles D'Orléans's strong-willed Feudal lord in "La Retenue d'Amors" ("Love's Retinue"). But owing to the Spanish preference for ecclesiastical parody, Juan Rodríguez's God of love is a parody of the God of Genesis, the Hebrew Yahweh. As the "Moses" of the courtly lovers, it is assumed that Juan Rodríguez has been chosen by the God of love to suffer the most from his love experience, because he and he alone will, by divine revelation, make known the will of the omnipotent to the unenlightened everywhere.

As the God of love ominously proclaims, there are grave penalties in store for the unfaithful who do not uphold his commandments. Yet these commandments, except for their number, bear little relation to the stone tablets of Mount Sinai, and an inspection of the former reveals their heretical nature:

El Primer Mandamiento	The First Commandment
El primero mandamiento, si mirays como dira, ¡quanto bien que vos sera de mi poco sentimiento! En tal lugar amaras do conoscas ser amado; no seras menospreciado de aquella que seruiras.	The first commandment, if you look closely at what it says, will bring you much profit as I clearly see it. You will only love where you are loved. You will not be scorned by her whom you serve.
Mirad que me contescio por seguir la voluntad, ofresci mi libertad a quien la menosprecio. El tienpo que la serui hasta auer conoscimiento de mis triste perdimiento, entiendo que lo perdi.	See what happened to me, for in following the dictates of my will I offered my freedom to a woman who scorned it. The time that I served her, until I became conscious of my sad loss, I now know was wasted.

Although a certain degree of realism must be assumed in the courtly love relationship (which is that the lady, being of a superior social status, may in fact have "chosen" her lover), the lover himself always felt honored to serve her, even if his love was not requited. Furthermore, any "joy" he derived from the love relationship was the result of his serving a spiritually superior being and restraining his own natural impulses, for then and only then could his love become "purified." And if he did suffer any pains in the process, he should have been content to do so. The first commandment, with its abrupt shift of narrators (from the God of love to the poet himself), is astonishing, for the advice is *not* to waste time on an ungrateful or hardhearted woman, which denies the very basis of the courtly love relationship: the assumed spiritual superiority of the lady. The apparent intention of this manual for courtly lovers, which is to spare them the pains of love, would consequently mean to deprive them of love's joys. Ultimately, therefore, "The Ten Commandments of Love" must be regarded as the advice of a cynic: that is, one who has been through the ordeal and now wishes to spare others a similar fate.

The second and third commandments stress the commonly accepted virtues of loyalty and chastity:

El Segundo

Al segundo luego vengo;
guardadlo como conuiene,
que por este se sostiene
lealtad, la qual mantengo.
Seras constante en amar
la señora que siruieres;
mientra que la mantouieres,
ella no te deue errar.

Quien galardon quiere auer
del seruicio que hiziere,
a la señora que siruiere
muy leal tiene de ser;
pues lealtad vos hara
venir al fin desseado,
quien amare siendo amado
con razon lo guardara.

The Second Commandment

To the second I now come;
observe this commandment properly,
which means being loyal,
and I am.
You will be constant in loving
the lady you serve;
as long as you keep this rule
she ought never to stray.

He who wishes a reward
for the service he performs
must be very loyal
to the lady he serves;
since loyalty will enable you
to attain the desired goal,
he who loves and is loved
with good reason keeps this rule.

El Tercero

El segundo es acabado;
donde 'l tercero comiença,
ocupar tiene vergüença
al que lo tiene passado.
Seras casto, no te mueua
tal codicia de trocar
la que tiene de guardar
por otra señora nueua.

¡O que derecha razon
es que pierda el que ganar
presume, por su mudar
do tiene su coraçon!
Pára mientes al cuydado
que nunca se partira
de quien lo recebira
dubda por auer errado.

The Third Commandment

The second has ended;
where the third begins
it is ashamed to assume the place
of the one previous;
you will be chaste
and not be tempted to exchange
the one you already have
for another passing fancy.

O how just it is
that he who thinks to win
should lose everything
because he was so fickle!
Take notice of the anxiety
that never leaves
a man who happily
deserted his beloved.

Loyalty, the necessary prerequisite for all the other virtues because of the relationship of courtly love to feudalism, is here nothing but a means to an end. Being loyal keeps one's lady faithful and helps gain the lady's confidence in order to attain the desired goal (*galardón* being an euphemism for the sex act).[1] Chastity for the Provençal troubadours was a relative term which implied a double standard of behavior. Since chastity was not the normal state of humans, it was assumed that both the lady and her vassal enjoyed physical lovemaking with others, but the love for one's lady was on a high spiritual plane and demanded a rational control of the senses. In effect, love created a state of joy (*jois*)[2] which by ennobling the lover, kept him faithful in that he did not serve more than one lady, for only she could inspire him with pure love (*Fin'Amors*). For Juan Rodríguez, however, chastity is a means of protecting one's honor. If the lover remains chaste, so will his lady, and the result is a kind of bargain in which the spiritual element is totally absent.

"The Fourth Commandment" begins the enumeration of the social virtues:

El Cuarto	The Fourth Commandment
Cessando de mas sonar	Ceasing further to resound,
el tercero que fenesce,	the third comes to an end,
pues el caso se me offesce,	but since the opportunity
del quarto vengo a tractar.	presents itself,
	I shall now treat the fourth.
Muestrate ser mesurado	Always be discreet
a todos generalmente	and pleasant to all in general
con alegre continente	if you wish to be well treated.
si quieres ser bien tractado.	
La mesura hallareys	Discretion you shall find
en las damas castellanas,	in Castilian ladies,
en especial seuillanas,	and especially those of Seville,
si tractar vos las quereys.	if you wish to enjoy their company.
Los que de aprender ouieron	Those who wish to learn anew
de nueuo ser mesurados,	how to be discreet,
cedo seran enseñados,	I admit that they will be instructed
si de aquestas aprendieren.	if they wish from the latter to learn.

For the Provençal troubadours, *mesura* meant "restraint," or "moderation" and was "a sign of the gentle heart."[3] It was perhaps the foremost courtly virtue, for it implied discretion, of paramount importance in an adulterous relationship. Love of one's lady also produced the virtues associated with youth (*jovens*), such as a happy disposition and generosity. Juan Rodríguez's advice, however, is to recommend that lovers be restrained and happy not as the result of the positive influence of love, but merely because that is the way to get on at court and be considered fit material to be loved. The allusion to the Castilian women, and the women of Seville in particular,[4] implies that these women prefer qualities in their lovers which the poet did not possess, and these were the qualities of the "successful" lovers at court.

The fifth and sixth commandments recommend bravery and truthfulness:

El Quinto

El quinto vengo diziendo,
una virtud que qualquier
puede bien amado ser
esta sola poseyendo.
Cura por ser esforçado,
que los que siguen amor,
deuen perder el temor,
pues es virtud ser osado.

De solo ser esforçados
se vos puede recrescer
tanto, que sin conoscer,
alcançareys ser amados.
Mirad como Ector fue
esforçado en la pelea,
por do la Pantasilea
sin lo ver, le dio su fe.

El Sesto

Del quinto mas no se lee;
de hablar va ya cessando:
el sesto viene mostrando

The Fifth Commandment

I come reciting the fifth,
a virtue for which, if he possess it,
any man can be well loved.
Try to be daring,
for those who are love's followers
should lose all fear
since it is a virtue
to be bold.

By merely being bold
so much can accrue to you
that, without knowing it,
you shall come to be loved.
Behold how Hector, daring in battle,
was beloved by Penthasileia,
who, without ever having seen him,
gave him her faith.

The Sixth Commandment

No more is read about the fifth,
one ceases to speak of it;
the sixth comes to show

las virtudes que posee:
sienpre seras verdadero,
que posseyendo tal fama,
te recebira tu dama
de grado por compañero.

Antes quiso fenescer
Regulo, consul romano,
en poder dell Africano,
que la verdad fallescer.
Pues nuestros antecessores
que fueron en otra edad
murieron por la verdad,
mantenedla vos, señores.

the virtues it possesses.
Always be truthful,
for possessing such a reputation,
your lady will gladly
receive you as her companion.

Regulus, the Roman consul,
wished rather to die
in the hands of the Africans
than not to keep his word.
Since our ancestors
who were of another age
died for the truth,
keep it, my lords.

As Robert B. Tate has shown, mythology and ancient history had a very special significance for fifteenth-century Spanish writers.[5] The Trojan Hector was an especially appealing figure, because the Trojan nation was considered civilized, brave, and outstanding in love. Regulus, the Roman consul, despite his rashness, was also a model for bravery, because he preferred to die at the hands of the Carthaginians, rather than to have Rome accept a humiliating peace during the Punic Wars.[6]

Continuing the list of the chivalric rather than the courtly virtues are the seventh and eighth commandments, which offer more advice on how to succeed in the world of the court:

El Seteno

El sesto se va dexando
de mas largo razonar;
al seteno da lugar
que se venga demonstrando.
Trabaja por te traer
ricamente con destreza,
qu' el amor con la probeza
mal se puede mantener.

Mirad bien en quanto grado
la riqueza fauoresce:
en la casa donde cresce,
del necio haze auisado:

The Seventh Commandment

The sixth no longer
keeps up its lengthy speech
and, as is seen,
gives way to the seventh.
Take special pains
to appear wealthy,
for love is difficult
to maintain with poverty.

See in what manner
wealth is an advantage
in the house
in which it grows:

assi por el consiguiente
donde no le plaze estar,
en breue haze tornar
al discreto imprudente.

it makes the simpleton discreet,
consequently, where it is not
it shortly makes the discreet
man imprudent.

El Octauo

Del seteno me despido,
el octauo començando,
mi processo acrescentando
de ciencia fallescido.
Fuyras la soledad,
beuiras en alegria,
buscando la compañía
parascera tu voluntad.

De beuir solo recrescen
grandes males sin medida,
y la fama destruyda
d' aquellos que lo padescen;
tristeza, poco saber,
desesperacion, oluido,
pensamiento desauido,
causan el seso perder.

The Eighth Commandment

I take leave of the seventh
to begin the eighth,
building up my method,
since I am lacking in knowledge.
You shall flee solitude
and live in joy,
and seeking the company of others
shall be your desire.

From living alone
result great ills without measure
and the reputation ruined
of those who suffer from it.
Melancholy, little wit,
desperation, forgetfulness and
distracted thoughts
caused one to lose one's sense.

The insistence upon dress as an outward sign of nobility is criticized by two contemporaries of Juan Rodríguez, Suero de Ribera and Hernando de Ludueña, both of whom composed manuals for courtly lovers similar to Juan Rodríguez's "Ten Commandments of Love."[7] For all three authors, dress was not only a means for making men more attractive to women, but it also distinguished the higher from the baser born.

The argument against solitude harkens back once more to the qualities needed by the "successful" courtier. High on the list would be gregariousness and a fondness for court social life. The often remarked "romantic" nature of the works of Juan Rodríguez is primarily the result of the poet's sense of alienation from the closed, tightly knit society of the Castilian court.

"The Ninth Commandment" is a valiant attempt to fuse the chivalric and courtly virtues:

El Noueno	The Ninth Commandment
El octauo queriendose retraer, el lugar de proponer al noueno traspassado; estudioso tu seras en obras de gentileza, con discrecion y destreza de la qual no partiras.	The eighth, having finished, wishes to withdraw and passes to make way for the ninth. You shall study works on good breeding and shall not deviate from the path of discretion and grace.
Gentileza hallaras en quien ama lealmente, y su propio continente quanto lo demandaras: nunca sigue en otra parte si no donde amor prospera, y alli se muestra bandera por los que siguen su arte.	Genteelness you shall find in him who loves faithfully and in his countenance however much you demand of it; he never looks elsewhere but where love prospers and wherever the banner is flown by the followers of his art.

What is meant precisely by "obras de gentileza" could translate roughly into modern English as "books of etiquette," primers in manners for social climbers. Thus, the courtly lover who wishes to have the appearance of an aristocrat despite his family origins must study the social refinements of the class he wishes to emulate, and if he does, according to Juan Rodríguez, he will prosper.

The tenth and final commandment recommends generosity:

El Dezeno	The Tenth Commandment
El noueno despedido, de todo lo processado, por dar fin a mi tractado soy al dezeno venido. Seras franco del querer; con todos auras cabida, y mayor de quien tu vida tiene en su libre poder.	The ninth, having taken leave of all that was said, I come to the tenth to give an end to my treatise. You will be generous in loving and will receive the confidence of all and especially of her who has your life in her power.
La virtud de la franqueza qualquier que la buscará, sepa que la hallará	The virtue of generosity, whoever shall seek it, know that it is to be found

donde gouierna nobleza.	where nobility governs.
Vayan al muy soberano	Go to the most sovereign
principe, rey de Castilla,	prince, the king of Castile,
que de la mas alto silla	who from the highest chair
la reparte con su mano.	dispenses it by his own hand.
A sus pies está mesura	At his feet lies moderation,
rigiendo toda su sala;	ruling the entire room;
a man izquierda, la gala,	at his left hand, pageantry;
de otro cabo, cordura,	on the other side, temperance
de semblante muy diuerso;	wearing a very different face;
sobre aquesta, discrecion,	above him, discretion,
alferez de su pendon,	the bearer of his colors,
gouernando el unierso.	governing the universe.

For the Provençal troubadours, generosity (*largueza*) was one of the virtues associated with youth and was inspired in a lover by his love and devotion for his lady. Here, on the other hand, generosity is only a means to an end, for it inspires confidence in a powerful lady who, almost literally, did hold her servant's life in her hands. The final two stanzas of this section are a blatant attempt at flattery, creating an allegorical scene in which the weak king, John II, presides over the court of the virtues of love.

The final stanza is a call to arms:

Fin	Finale
Toca, toca caualgar;	Sound the trumpets for the charge,
essos trompetas clarones	those clarion trumpets sound,
desembueluan los pendones,	and the colors unfurl;
yremos a pelear	we go to fight
con todos los condenados	all the condemned,
perdidos por eregia,	damned by their heresy
que mantouieron profia	who struggled against
contra Amor y sus criados.	the God of love and his host.

The final scene exemplifies the crusading fervor of the era, when nearly all the Christians of Spain were preparing to oust the Moors from Granada and fulfill their supposedly historical mission. Despite its crusading message, the final stanza is ironic, for all of the rules espoused by the "prophet" run counter to the spirit and letter of the courtly love "law," which held that the joys of love arose from the elevating power of service to a lady, superior to the male socially and spiritually.

By creating a series of commandments to avoid unhappiness in love, the poet portrays the court society of his era as being fit not for the true courtly lover but for the courtier, the hypocrite, and social climber interested only in the appearance of courtly love. "The Ten Commandments of Love" is a cynical work, but it does show the author's awareness of what courtly love should have been and what it was not in Castile. It is well known that in later eras, many a Castilian noble who wished to rise at court might do so by pretending to be from the upper nobility. It is also well known that many a Castilian lady wished to meet and marry only a member of the upper nobility, and that Castilian women in general preferred (at least in literature, and especially popular literature)[8] the chivalric virtues (courage, military prowess) to the courtly ones. Juan Rodríguez's "Ten Commandments of Love" may be interpreted then as an indictment of a society which did not understand courtly love, and, as a Galician and a foreigner, he had a superior capacity for judgment. It was Juan Rodríguez's right to proclaim himself the "Moses" of the courtly love movement, but the Moses of "The Ten Commandments of Love" is a cynical prophet who reveals the bankruptcy of his god and the sad state of his religion.

As was mentioned previously, any realism in the literature of this era was possible only after strict adherence to elaborate formalities. In "The Ten Commandments of Love," the convention to be honored is allegory itself. Before offering his criticisms, Juan Rodríguez must first present the God of love in full Jehovah-like splendor, then put words in his mouth which mock the true spirit of the religion of love. While "The Ten Commandments of Love" is not nearly so ambitious as "The Seven Joys of Love," perhaps because it is not aimed directly at the lady herself but at love in general, nonetheless, it is a decalogue of what love should have been and, simultaneously, what

it was not. For, on the one hand, the thunderous words of
Jehovah proclaim that the Children of Israel have replaced
their Lord with the Golden Calf. The so-called courtly lovers
must be led away from their wicked ways, and only the true
prophet of love, Juan Rodríguez, can do this. On the other hand,
the God of love is cynical himself, as he shows that successful
lovers at the court are not the real courtly lovers, but only
those who feign courtliness.

CHAPTER 4

Minor Poems

I *"Ham, ham, huyd que rauio"*
("Grr, Grr, Flee, for I Rage")

IN this highly unusual little poem, the poet claims to have been turned into a howling dog by the force of his passion and the sense of frustration he feels at not being able to reveal the identity of the author of his woes—his lady. Thus he can express his rage only by howling:

Ham, ham, huyd que rauio
con rauia, de vos no traue,
por trauar de quien agrauio
recibo tal y tan graue.

Si yo rauio por amar,
esto no sabran de mi,
que del todo enmudeci,
que no se si no ladrar,
Ham, ham, huyd que rauio.
¡O quien pudiese trauar
de quien me haze ell agrauio
y tantos males passar!

Ladrando con mis cuidados,
mil veces me viene a mientes
de lançar en mi los dientes
y me comer a bocados.
Ham, ham, huyd que rauio.
Aullad, pobres sentidos;
pues os hacen tal agrauio,
dad mas fuertes alaridos.

Grr, grr, flee, for I rage,
and beware that I don't bite you
in attempting to bite the one
who has so sorely outraged me.

If I rage for love,
they will never discover this from me,
for I have concealed everything
and all I can do is rage.
Grr, grr, flee, for I rage.
O, if I could only bite
the one who outrages me
and makes me suffer such torment!

Barking aloud with my woes,
a thousand times it has occurred
   to me
to thrust my own teeth in me
and devour myself by mouthfuls.
Grr, grr, flee, for I rage.
Howl, you poor senses,
since they so outrage you,
howl all the louder.

Cabo	Finale
No cessando de rauiar,	Never ceasing to rage
no digo si por amores,	I do not say whether for love,
no valen saludadores,	but doctors are of no help,
ni las ondas la mar.	nor are the waves of the sea.
Ham, ham, huyd que raio.	Grr, grr, flee, for I rage.
Pues no cumple declarar	Since I canot declare
la causa de tal agrauio,	the cause of such an outrage,
el remedio es el callar.	the only remedy is to keep still.

Although at first glance this image may appear bizarre, or even grotesque, it should be remembered that one of the profoundest images in medieval literature is that of the lover turned into a wild man or savage by the intensity of his passion and a feeling of rejection by his lady.[1] Many were the knights who, because of what we might call a temporary madness, sought refuge in the forest to escape the glances and intrigues of the court. Even Merlin himself, under the spell of an enchantress, was known to roam about dressed in skins. Such a transformation, far from discrediting the knight, did him honor, for there were positive associations with this state. Learned men would equate the fates of the knights in the forest with the lives of saints such as St. John Crysostom, who went off to the forest, dwelt as a hermit, was tempted by the flesh, and emerged victorious. It was always assumed that when the knight dwelt in the forest as a wild man he still remained his lady's loyal vassal, and sought willingly to return to her whenever he could get back into favor.

The originality of "Ham, ham, huyd que rauio" lies in the fact that the poet is converted not into a wild man but into a howling dog or possibly a wolf. The use of this image transports us out of the realm of chivalric literature into the world of Galician-Celtic folklore, with its tales of *meigas* or witches who could turn men into *lobishomes* ("werewolves") or howling dogs.[2] As we said previously in relation to "Seven Joys of Love," Provençal courtly love presupposed that woman's power or "magic" was benevolent, and would not only elevate man spiritually, but even grant him great physical powers in battle. When woman's power is malevolent, as it appears to be in

"Ham, ham, huyd que rauio," then the male is rendered powerless, and the best that can be said of the poet's current state is
that once more he wishes to be known as a martyr for love. As
strange as it may seem, his current state (that of a howling dog
or wolf), "marks" him as a superior being, capable of "pure" or
courtly love, for his frustration (that is, his inability to reveal
his lady's identity), has led to his remarkable physical transformation. The uniqueness of "Ham, ham, huyd que rauio" is that
it brings the world of forest with its transformations and wild
creatures into the province of the court.

II *"Solo por uer a Macías"* (*"Only to See Macías"*)

Each in its own way, "Grr, Grr, Flee, for I Rage" and "Only
to See Macías" are precursors of Juan Rodríguez's sentimental
novel, *Siervo libre de amor.* While the former poem deals with
the lover's transformation from a rational being to howling dog
because of intense frustration and passion, the latter, by means
of ecclesiastical parody, deals with a voyage to the underworld,
a necessary prerequisite for many heroes of epic literature. In
"Only to see Macías," the poet considers himself as wanting to test his lady's affections by imagining his own death and
subsequent resurrection:

Solo por uer a Macias	Only to see Macías
de amor me partir,	and take leave of love,
yo me querria morir,	I had wished to die
con tanto que resurgir	so that in three days hence
pudiese dende a tres dias.	I could be risen.
Mas luego que resurgiese	But as soon as I were to rise,
¿quien me podria tener	who, o lovely lady,
que en mi mortaja non fuese,	who was not in my shroud, could
lynda sennora, a te uer,	restrain me
por uer que planto farias,	when I saw you,
sennora, o que reyr?	in order to see what lamenting
yo me querria morir,	you would make, my love,
con tanto que resurgir	or what laughter?
podiese dende a tres dias.	I had wished to die, so that
	in three days hence I could be risen.

Although the poem is very playful, the poet has once more established his link with Macías, the foremost martyr for love. From the choice of imagery, we can easily deduce that Juan Rodríguez has again laid claim to being courtly love's only true messiah, for the life and death of Macías augured the coming of the true redeemer of love, just as the life and death of John the Baptist prefigured the coming of Christ.

III *"Tan fuertes llamas d' amor"* (*"Such Strong Flames of Love"*)

Continuing his use of ecclesiastical parody, the poet argues that so great is his suffering for love that, like Christ, were he to die, the world would be cleansed of pain and suffering:

Tan fuertes llamas d' amor
trebajan la vide mia
no te viendo,
que sin pena a sin dolor
todo el mundo quedaria,
yo muriendo.

Such strong flames of love
torment my life
when I do not see you,
that all the world
would without pain or torment be
were I to die.

Congoxa, dolor, tormento,
e quantas penas sentir
por amor e comedir
se podrian, yo las siento.
De tanto mal sofridor
cada ora a cada dia
soy biuiendo,
que sin pena a sin dolor
todo 'l mundo quedaria,
yo muriendo.

Anguish, pain and torment
and all the suffering
that could be felt
for love and chivalry
I do feel.
I love with so much suffering
every hour and every day
that all the world
would without pain and torment be
were I to die.

¡O muerte, singular gloria,
viniendo, me puedes dar,
que pueda 'l mundo dexar
sin pena por mi memoria!
Biuo tan triste amador
la tu cruel señoria
atendiendo,
que sin pena e sin dolor
todo 'l mundo quedaria,
yo muriendo.

O death, your coming
would bring me singular glory,
for I might leave the world
without suffering
because of its memory of me!
I live as such a sad lover
awaiting your cruel reign
that all the world
would without pain and torment be
were I to die.

In the works of Juan Rodríguez, ecclesiastical parody is a literary device which appears to be the product of his early works. The above work is the last poem we shall discuss which makes use of ecclesiastical parody as the sole basis of a work. Henceforth, fresh ideas appear which mark a new maturity, culminating in prose works such as his sentimental novel, *Siervo libre de amor*. The image of the lover's suffering as capable of "redeeming" the world, or, at the least, the world of courtly lovers, is one that has been termed "romantic" by critics who no doubt saw a precursor of the famous romantic image of the satanic hero redeemed by the love of a pure maiden. Only in this case, the *agnus dei* ("sacrificial lamb") of love is a male rather than a female martyr, as was usually the case in the nineteenth century. "Such Strong Flames of Love" harkens back directly to "Seven Joys of Love" and looks beyond it, for while the latter described the events which led to the lover's "passion," the former foretells all lovers' "redemption."

IV *"Bien amar, leal seruir"* (*"To Love Well and Serve Loyally"*)

At certain stages of any love relationship, including courtly love, the lover may feel that his service is in vain, and this is what is expressed in "Bien amar, leal seruir":

Bien amar, leal seruir,	To love well and serve loyally,
cridar et decir mis penas,	shout and declare my suffering
es sembrar en las arenas	is to sow in the desert
o en las ondas escreuir.	or write upon the waves.
Si tanto quanto serui	If for all that I had served
sembrara en la ribera,	I had planted on the shore,
tengo reuerdesciera	I declare that the latter would bloom
et diera fructo de si.	and bear fruit.
E aun por uerdat dezir,	And truly I admit
sy yo tanto escreuiera	that if I were to write as much
en la mar, yo bien podiera	in the sea, well could I
todas las ondas tennir.	all the waters stain.

Although the image employed was rather a stereotyped one in the late Middle Ages, that of the strength of one's passion

being capable of bringing life to barrenness or staining the
waters of the sea, students of English literature will recall the
famous lines of Shakespeare's Macbeth: "This hand would/
The multitudinous seas incarnadine,/ Making the green one
red."[3]

V *"Biue leda si podras"* (*"Live Happily If You Can"*)

Although there is no conclusive biographical evidence, it has
usually been assumed that "Live Happily If You Can" and "Muy
triste sera mi uida" (to appear below) were written as a reaction
to the poet's enforced exile. Both poems achieved a bit of fame
in their time, especially the former:[4]

Biue leda si podras
e non penes atendiendo,
que segund peno partiendo,
non espero que iamas
te uere nin me ueras.

¡O dolorosa partida!
¡Triste amador, que pido
licencia, et me despido
de tu uista et de mi uida!
El trabajo perderas
en auer de mi mas cura,
que segund mi grand tristura,
non espero que jamas
te uere nin me ueras.

Live happily if you can
and do not suffer by waiting,
for as I suffer in departing,
I expect never to see you
nor you to see me.

O dolorous departure!
A sad lover is he who begs
leave to depart
from your sight and from his very
life!
You will waste your time
in thinking about me,
for because of my great sadness,
I never expect to see you
nor you to see me.

The emotion rendered is *saudade,* practically impossible to
translate into English except by saying that it is a feeling of
nostalgia or sadness evoked by the memory of one's lady who
is far away.[5] It is an emotion peculiar to Galician-Portuguese
poetry and uniquely absent from Castilian courtly love verse.

VI *"Muy triste sera mi uida"* (*"How Sad My Life Shall Be"*)

Similar in feeling, but not as tender, is "How Sad My Life
Shall Be":

Muy triste sera mi uida	How sad my life shall be
los dias que non vos viere;	the days I do not see you,
y mi persona vencida	and my person, overcome
del dolor de la partida,	by the pain of the departure,
morira quando muriere.	shall die when we would be reunited.
Biuiran los pensamientos	The thoughts I had of you
que con vos siempre e tenido;	shall always live;
no moriran los tormentos	the torments given undeservedly
dados sin mereçimientos	which I received from you
que de vos he resciuido.	shall never die.
Y asi sera conocido	And so it shall be known,
mi vida quanto vos quiere;	my life, how much you were loved;
y mi persona vencida	and my person, overcome
del dolor de la partida,	by the pain of the departure,
morira quando muriere.	shall die when we would be reunited.

Rather than dwelling on the feeling of nostalgia or *saudade,* "How Sad My Life Shall Be" returns to the theme of the lover's death as a result of the pains of love, which bring him everlasting fame through martyrdom. Resorting once again to casuistry, there is a play on words with *pensamientos,* which implied not merely "thoughts," but "dark, passionate thoughts or obsessions."[6]

VII   *"Fuego del diuino rayo"* (*"Fire of the Divine Ray"*)

In the early fifteenth century, it was not uncommon for a poet who had spent his early years writing verses to his lady to repent his actions and claim that his former life was sin and folly. Thus there arose the subgenre known as the *palinodio* ("palinode"), in which the poet would bid a final, fond farewell to the court and worldly pleasures, and promise to lead a saintly, ascetic life in order to find salvation lest it be too late:

Fuego del diuino rayo,	Fire of the divine ray,
dolce flama syn ardor,	sweet flame that does not sting,
esfuerço contra desmayo,	courage against despair,
remedio contra dolor,	remedy against pain,
alumbra tu seruidor.	enlighten your servant.
La falsa gloria del mundo	I have contemplated the false glory
e vana prosperidat	and vain prosperity of the world,

contemplé;
con pensamiento profundo
el centro de su maldat
penetré.
Oyga quien es sabidor
el planto de la serena,
la qual, temiendo la pena
de la tormenta mayor,
plañe en el tiempo mejor.

Asy yo, preso de espanto,
que la diuina virtud
offendi,
comienço mi triste planto
fazer en mi iuuentud
desde aqui;
los desiertos penetrando,
do con esquiuo clamar
pueda, mis culpas llorando,
despedirme syn temor,
de falso plazer e honor.

Fin

Adios, real esplandor
que yo serui et loé
coin lealtat;
adios, que todo el fauor
e cuanto de amor fablé
es uanidat.
Adios, los que bien amé;
adios, mundo engañador;
adios, donas que ensalcé
famosas, dignas de loor,
orad por mí pecador!

and with profound thinking
have penetrated
the core of its evil.
He who is wise,
let him heed
the song of the siren
who, fearing the pain
of the storm,
laments in time of calm.

Thus I, gripped with fear,
I who have offended
the divine virtue,
do begin to make
my sad lament now,
in my youth,
so that I, entering
the deserts
may with secret cries bemoan my
    guilt
and depart, without fear,
from false pleasure and honor.

Finale

Farewell, royal splendor
which I loyally served and praised.
Farewell, for whatever
I spoke of love
and good fortune is vanity.
Farewell, you whom I loved well.
Farewell, deceitful world;
farewell, you ladies
whom I exalted,
famous ladies, worthy of praise,
pray for me, your sinner.

In late thirteenth-century Provençal poetry, the figure who replaced the lady as the object of praise and devotion was the Virgin herself,[7] and in medieval Spain, also, poets writing in Galician, including King Alphonse the Wise, would pledge themselves to serve the Virgin when they grew disillusioned with love.[8] For these reasons, Juan Rodríguez is perfectly within the tradition of turning to the Savior's Mother when courtly love had lost its appeal. However, despite the medieval commonplaces strung together—*memento mori* ("remember death"), *vanitas vanitatem* ("vanity of vanities") and *sic transiunt gloriae mundi* ("thus pass the glories of the world"), there is an element of insincerity about the poem which is evident in the finale. Despite his eagerness to repent, the poet seems proud to have loved well and achieved some fame in addition, and we must conclude that the finale, rather than giving the reader a sense of true repentance, seems to be the author's way of boasting about his accomplishments.

VIII *"Debate de Alegria e del Triste Amante"* (*"The Debate between Happiness and the Sad Lover"*)

In terms of chronology, it is generally agreed that Juan Rodríguez's poetry predates his prose, which was written in the period ca. 1438–ca. 1450.[9] His poetry, however, has never been divided into stages, either thematically or chronologically, and we feel that this calls for a reevaluation. Whether "Debate de Alegria e del Triste Amante," and the poems to follow, "Planto de Pantasilea," "O desuelada, sandia" and the chivalric ballads postdate the other nine poems discussed above cannot as yet be determined; however, there is some internal evidence to suggest a different, maturer attitude on the part of the poet, who begins to turn away from ecclesiastical parody and casuistry as literary devices to concentrate more on dramatic effects such as monologues or, as is the case in "Debate," a sentimental-philosophical dialogue in which "Happiness" tries to convince "the Sad Lover" to abandon his cause:

–No huys,	"Do not flee,
en vuestra busca soy venida,	I am come to help you."
–A mi dezis?	"Me, you say?
dexatme, au' ya es perdida	Leave me, for my freedom is lost,
ibertat, la qual tenia,	(which I used to have)
por trabajarme	in trying to follow
de seguir a quien porfia	the one who sought
por matarme.	to slay me."
–No me conoceys,	"You answer thus

pues respondés assi.
—No me culpeys,
pues no se parte de mi;
qu' el mi gran desseo
es tan fuerte,
por el qual bien veo
ya mi muerte.
—Yo soy alegria
que vos vengo a consolar.
—Ya passó el dia
que vos anduve buscar.
—Yo era vuestro servidor;
vos os partistes.
—Desque fuy buen amador,
nunca boluistes.
—Pues que vengo
queret me luego tomar.
—Tanto mal tengo,
catiuo por bien amar,
c' alçar mis oios agora,
no vos puedo;
mas de mi fin sabidora
sereys çedo.
—Si quereys vuestra fin
es escusado.
Mal lo sabeys
quant' os es bien allegado.
—Va, bien es muy mejor
que no biuir,
quien tan esquiuo dolor
ha de sofrir.
—Seguir mi via,
vida sera para vos.
—Bien seria,
mas no puede ser, par Dios.
Obligueme con simpleza
de seruir
por quien ha hombre tristeza
de morir.
—Poco entendeys,
pues de mi os apartays.
—Vos no veys
de que guisa me tomays;

because you don't know me."
"Do not blame me,
for I no longer
am myself,
for my passion is so strong
that I see my death
approaching."
"I am Happiness
come to console you."
"The day is gone
when I have sought you out."
"I was your servant
then you departed."
"When I became a true lover
you never returned."
"Since I am come now,
embrace me."
"So much do I suffer
being a slave for love,
that I cannot lift my eyes now
to face you.
But I am sure that you know
what will be my fate."
"If you wish your demise,
that is excusable.
Little do you know
how much good is in store for you."
"Leave me,
for it is better
for him not to live
who suffers such terrible pain."
"Follow me
and you will live."
"I should like to,
but it cannot be, by God,
for I foolishly pledged myself
to serve her
who makes one
sad unto death."
"You understand very little
since you avoid me."
"You do not know
what shape I'm in.

qu' en verdat much cerquno
de partida
que haure de fazer temprano
desta vida.
—El partimiento
¿no me direys quien lo aquexa?
—Pensamiento
continuo que no me dexa;
que nunca tales dolores
padezio
hombre triste por amores
como yo.
—Si escapays,
seguireys luego mis vias?
—Demas fablays,
pues son tan pocos mis dias;
mas si alguna vida oviere
por ventura,
seguire quanto pudiere
la tristura.
—Soy seguro
de vos aver menester;
mas ante la muerte venga
a me partir,
por que tal pena non me tenga
de seguir.
—A tanto mal
quien vos fizo ser llegado?
—Desigual
amor muy desordenado
que me tiene en su poder,
e me faze
toda pena padescer
que le plaze.
—Yo me despido
de vos en quanto vivierdes.
—Yo soy perdido;
fazed el mal que quisierdes,
no hay danyo mas peor
que cobrar tal desfauor
del qual muero.

For in truth
I will soon be
taking leave
of this life."
      "This departure,
will you tell me who is hastening it?"
      "An obsession
which does not leave me,
for never did any man
who was saddened by love
suffer
as much as I."
      "If you escape,
will you follow my path?"
      "You are too prolix,
and my days are so short;
but if by chance I had some life to
      live,
I would follow, as much as I
were able,
the path of Sadness."
      "I am sure
I will need you."
      "But do it before death comes
to take me away,
because such pain
will not follow me."
      "Who brought you to
such suffering?"
      "Great
and powerful Love
who has me in his power
and who makes me suffer
as much pain
as he pleases."
      "I say farewell to you
for as long as you live."
      "I am lost;
do all the evil you wish,
for there is no harm worse
than to be out of favor
with the one who causes my death."

Fin	Finale
Por buen señor	As a good knight
a mi fin soy llegado,	I am come to my end
en mas honor	with more honor
que cauteloso namorado.	than were I a cautious lover.

Despite its title, "Debate" is not a true "debate" in that formal rules are not followed and no "court" is asked to judge the winner. Rather, the work seems to be a dramatic poem, a forerunner of the most famous dramatic poem of the fifteenth century, Rodrigo Cota's "Diálogo entre el Amor y un Viejo" ("Dialogue between Love and an Old Man").[10] In Cota's poem, Love comes to visit an old man in the latter's garden in order to persuade him to accept love. The old man, having reached the point of physical decay as well as disillusionment with past experiences, at first greets Love harshly, but later is seduced by his arguments. After symbolically embracing Love, the old man suddenly feels all the former amorous desires and torments in his body. At this point, Love turns on him and humiliates him, bequeathing him the following punishment: he will fall in love with a hardhearted young girl who will never fall in love with him. The poem ends with the old man begging Love for forgiveness. Like Cota's work, Juan Rodríguez's poem is also a short, dramatic scene, but whereas Cota's work was a warning against the evils of love, Juan Rodríguez's "Debate" argues that the state of a "true" lover is unhappiness, and that the temptations of happiness can only deprive him of the rewards to be gained by martyrdom.

At first glance, "Debate" appears to be an eloquent defense of the principles of Provençal courtly love as understood in the fifteenth century, in which the lover's "joy" sprang from being denied the fruits of physical lovemaking so that he could earn the right to be the lady's "true" lover in the spiritual sense. Thus, by definition, "joy" meant being in a constant state of frustration, and no "true" lover could call himself happy if he satisfied his physical needs to the detriment of his spiritual relationship with his lady. With this in mind then, in terms of the logic of "Debate," yielding to happiness (that is, satisfying the needs of *homo naturalis*, the "natural man") meant yielding to the voice of the devil, for once having yielded, the fruits of the lover's paradise would forever be denied.

In terms of maturation of thought, "Debate" appears to represent a later stage in the thinking of Juan Rodríguez, for even though the poem is still a variation on the same theme—his attempt to gain immortality as a martyr for love—there does appear a thought which will be reiterated in his sentimental novel, *Siervo libre de amor* (*The Emancipated Slave of Love*), which is that the true servant or slave of love never ceases to be a lover (in a spiritual sense), even when the love relationship may have ended (for whatever reasons).[11] A note of this new maturity is the rather subdued (for Juan Rodríguez at least) ending in which he speaks of attaining "more honor" than had he been a cautious lover, yet no grandiose martyrdom or voyage to the underworld is depicted or alluded to. Another hint of the poem's being a precursor of *Siervo libre de amor* is that henceforth he must follow the "path of sadness," for the lover is changed by love and becomes a new person. In Juan Rodríguez's case, this will mean a long spiritual journey in the form of an allegory in the second part of *Siervo libre de amor*. As can be seen from "Debate," the dialogue does not produce a completely satisfactory ending, for the poet claims to be "lost" even though his honor is intact. It is apparent that simple martyrdom by means of ecclesiastical parody no longer suffices. From this point on, all dilemmas will have to be worked out in the world outside of the court, using figures drawn from ancient mythology, the chivalresque ballads, or from new characters invented by the author himself.

IX "*Planto de Pantasilea*" ("*Pantasilea's Lament*")

Until the publication of recent articles by Alessandra Bartolini[12] and Charles H. Leighton,[13] "Planto de Pantasilea" was generally attributed to the Marqués de Santillana,[14] although there was little evidence to support the claim.[15] In this work, the Amazon queen, Pantasilea, comes to lament the death of Hector. Pantasilea is perhaps the most unusual of Juan Rodríguez's characters, for in her he has combined the ideal knight and the ideal lady. In that she is an Amazon warrior fighting

many fierce tribes to come to her beloved, Pantasilea is mascu-
line; in that she falls in love with Hector by hearsay and prays
to Venus directly, she is feminine. Pantasilea laments Hector's
death in the sentimental rather than heroic tradition, for she
insists repeatedly that she will be remembered not as the greatest
warrior but as the greatest martyr for love, much in the manner
of her creator:

Yo sola membrança sea,	May I be the sole memory
enxiemplo a todas personas:	and example to all persons;
la triste Pantasilea,	I, the sad Penthasileia,
reyna de las amazonas;	queen of the Amazons;
Ector, que gloria posea,	Hector, may his soul be in heaven,
ame, por donde muriese;	I loved, because of which I died;
el triste, que amar desea,	the sad one, who wishes to love,
ya mi planto e fin oyese.	let him hear my sad lament and death.

As was mentioned above, Pantasilea falls in love with Hector
by reputation and not by sight, proving one of the tenets of the
God of love in "The Ten Commandments of Love":[16]

Por fama fuy enamorada	By reputation I fell in love
del que non vi en mi vida;	with him whom I never saw.
por armas venci, cuytada!	By arms I conquered, unhappy wo-
e fuy por fama vencida....	man that I am!
	And I was conquered by reputa-
	tion....

Under the principles of courtly love, the God of love is
invincible, and even the queen of the Amazons is powerless
against him:

en estorias quantas leo	In all the tales I read
non falle quien me venciese,	I never found anyone who
salvo Amor e buen deseo	could defeat me except love and
de un solo que bien quiesiese.	desire
	of only one whom I loved well.

In "Pantasilea's Lament" are two figures found frequently in
fifteenth-century courtly love poetry which are not found in
Juan Rodríguez's other poems—Venus and Fortune:

Venus, ¿do tanto servicio	Venus, where is all the service
que te fize atribulada?	that I in my hour of need gave you?
de oracion e sacrificio	What profit have I earned
que galardon he sacado?	from all the prayers and sacrifice?

quando reynar atendia,	When I expected to rule,
la rueda bolvio Fortuna.	Fortune turned the Wheel.

The wheel of fortune, as scholars have shown, acquired importance in the fourteenth century and remained important in the fifteenth because of the political upheavals and period of adjustment from the Middle Ages to the Renaissance.[17]

As in other poems by Juan Rodríguez, when the lover is unable to attain his goals, he ends by seeking death, and Pantasilea does likewise:

De la grand pena que avia,	Because of the great pain I had,
lo mas que me consolava	what consoled me most
era: que presto morria,	was that I would quickly die
segund el mal que passava.	because of the ill I was suffering.

In point of fact, Pantasilea did not die of love but was slain, like Hector, by Achilles. Indirectly, however, it may be said that by rushing to Hector's aid and dying at the hands of Achilles also, Pantasilea did indeed die for love and thus merits being called either a heroine or martyr for love, and her tragico-sentimental death does much to remind Juan Rodríguez's reading public of the latter's own love story.

Pantasilea is Juan Rodríguez's great egalitarian figure in the battle for equality of the sexes in the courtly love relationship. She does not passively dominate by virtue of superior status, as do the women of the court. Out in the field of battle, away from the artificiality of the court, love has little to do with social rank or assigned, stereotypical roles. Away from the court, the differences in gender between Ardanlier, the protagonist of the third section of *Siervo libre de amor*, and Pantasilea will mean very little.

CHAPTER 5

Poems of Controversy

I Three Chivalric Ballads

AS David W. Foster has shown,[1] the Spanish ballad occupies a much more important role in the history of Spanish literature than does the ballad of other European countries. Rather than being a mere object of anthropological study, as are the ballads of England and France, Spanish authors from the fifteenth to the twentieth centuries have copied the ballad style and written their own individual ballads on themes which are part of the ballad repertoire. The humble ballad, therefore, was almost never an object of scorn,[2] even by court poets who wished to show their erudition.

However, before continuing, let us pause to discuss the problems connected with assigning the authorship of a ballad to any one individual. When the romantic writers of the early nineteenth century rebelled against the rigidity of neoclassicism, they turned to a study of pre-Christian religion, art, and folk customs. Thus, they came to admire the ballad and to consider it a *Volkslied* or "people's song," the product, not of a single artist, but of an anonymous group, such as an entire community. Later in the nineteenth century, French critics imbued with the spirit of positivism turned away from the romantic idea of group authorship and argued for the individual artist as the only possible author of the ballad. From the early twentieth century to the present, Ramón Menéndez Pidal and his followers have proposed an intermediate theory known as "Traditionalism," which claims that the first ballads in Spain, the *romances históricos* or "historical ballads" were reworked fragments of long, epic poems either wholly composed or, at least, transmitted and modified by *juglares* or minstrels who sang

72

them in the open markets and squares. Problems of authorship grow even more difficult when it is remembered that each ballad usually has several variants which are often similar but not identical. Thus, nearly all the ballads discovered in the fifteenth century dealing with certain themes are thought to have been composed by these anonymous minstrels, especially if they display certain stylistic traits which all ballads have in common, such as the sixteen-syllable line divided into two octosyllabic hemistichs and a kind of speech known as "formulistic diction," which repeats certain phrases for particular effects.[3]

When Hugo Rennert first published the contents of a British Museum manuscript in 1893,[4] there were, among other works, three ballads dealing with chivalric themes found among other poems attributed to Juan Rodríguez.[5] Largely on the basis of intuition, Rennert chose to accept Juan Rodríguez as their probable author rather than collector,[6] but critics who were contemporaries of Rennert, such as the venerable Menéndez y Pelayo,[7] were dubious. Today controversy still rages as to whether Juan Rodríguez is their author, their "reworker," or simply their collector. It is our opinion that Juan Rodríguez is the probable author of two of these ballads and may have composed the third, although there is less proof for assigning *La hija del rey de Francia* to him than the other works.

A "Rosaflorida"

Before beginning our analysis, we have decided to place before the reader two versions of the ballads: the one found in the British Museum manuscript, which we shall refer to as the London version, and the *Cancionero de romances de Amberes* (*The Ballad Songbook of Amsterdam*), which we shall refer to as the Amsterdam version:

London	London
Allá en aquella ribera	Upon the shore
que se llama de Ungria,	which is Hungary called
alli estaba un castillo	stands a castle
que se llamaba Chapiua	named Chapiva,
dentro estaba una donzella	and there within a damsel lay

que se llama Rosaflorida:
siete condes la demandan,
tres reyes de Lunbardia;
todos los a deseñado,
tanta es la su loçania.
Enamoróse de Montesinos
de oydas, que no de vista,
a faza la media noche
vozes de Rrosaflorida:
oydo lo abie Blandinos,
el su ayo que tenia,
levantarse corriendo
de la cama do dormia.
¿Qué abedes vos, la Rrosa?
¿qué abedes Rrosaflorida?
Que en las vozes que dades
pareces loca sandia.
Ay, fablo la donzella
bien oyres lo que diria:
ay bien vengas tu, Blandinos,
bien sea la tu venida,
llebesme aquesta carta,
de sangre la tengo escrita
llebesmela á Montesinos,
á las tierras do bivia,
que me viniese á vere
para la Pascua Florida;
por dineros no lo dexe,
yo pagare la venida;
vestire los sus rapazes
de una seda broslida;
Si mas quiere Montesinos
yo much mas le daria,
dalle yo trynta castillos,
Todos rriberas de Ungria;
si mas quiere Montesinos,
yo mucho mas la daria;
dalle yo cien marcos d' oro,
otros tantos de plata fina;
si mas quiere Montesinos
yo mucho mas le daria;
dalle yo cien marcos d'oro,
otros tantos de plata fina;

by name, Rosaflorida.
By seven counts her hand was
    sought,
by three kings of Lombardy,
but so haughty and so proud was she
that all they were disdainèd.
In love with Montesinos she fell,
by fame and not by sight,
and then toward midnight
could be heard Rosaflorida calling
    out.
Overheard by Blandinos was she,
Blandinos her tutor.
He rose and quickly to her ran
from the bed in which he lay
    sleeping.
"What is the matter, sweet Rose,"
    said he,
"What is it, Rosaflorida?
For by your shouting
it's mad you seem."
"Alas," said the maid,
"mark well what I am saying.
O Blandinos it's glad I am
for your coming.
Now take this letter
all written in blood
and take it to Montesinos.
Take it to the land
wherein he dwells
and tell him to see me at Easter.
For money let him not despair,
for I shall pay his expenses.
And I will dress in finest silk
every one of his pages,
and if it's more that he shall want,
it's more that I shall give him.
For I shall give him castles thirty,
all on Hungary's shore,
And if Montesinos wishes more,
it's more that I shall give him.
Thirty marks of gold shall be his
and another thirty in silver.

si mas quiere Montesinos
yo mucho mas le daria;
dalle yo este me cuerpo
siete años a la su gusa
que sy dél no se pagare
que tome su mejoria.

And if Montesinos wishes more
it's more that I shall give him.
One hundred marks in gold shall
   be his
and another one hundred in silver,
and if Montesinos wishes more
much more shall I give him.
This body shall I give to him
to use seven years however he
   wishes.
And if this be not payment enough,
let him take whatever he wishes.

Amsterdam

En Castilla está un castillo
que se llama Rocafrida;
al castillo llaman Roca
y á el fonte llaman Frida.
El pié tenia de oro,
y almenas de plata fina;
entre almena y almena
está una piedra zafira:
tanto relumbra de noche
como el sol á medio dia.
Dentro estaba una doncella
que llaman Rosaflorida:
siete condes la demandan,
tres duques de Lombardia;
á todos les desdeñaba,
tanta es su lozania.
Enamoróse de Montesinos
de oidas, que no de vista.
Una noche estando así,
gritos de Rosaflorida;
oyérala un camarero,
que en su camara dormia.
¿Qué es aquesto, mi señora?
¿qúé es esto, Rosaflorida?
ó tenedes mal de amores,
ó estáis loca, sandia,
mas llevásesme estas cartas
á Francia la bien guardnia;
diés las á Montesinos,

Amsterdam

There is a castle in Castile
which is called Rocafrida;
the castle is "Roca" by name,
and the fountain is "frida."
The base is of solid gold
and the ramparts of finest silver,
Between the battlements is a
   sapphire stone
which shines all night
like the sun in the daylight bright.
Within a damsel lay,
Rosaflorida by name.
Seven counts seek her hand
and three dukes of Lombardy.
And so proud is she
that each one does she scorn.
She fell in love with Montesinos
by fame and not by sight.
But so in love was she one night
that all could hear her shout,
and hastened there a chamberlain
who in her chamber there did sleep.
"What's this, my lady?
What's this, my Rosaflorida?
Either it's in love you be
or you're completely mad."
"O take these letters to France," says
   she,
"to France so rich and hearty,

la cosa que (yo) mas queria;	and give them there to Montesinos,
dile que ne venga á ver	the man I love most dearly.
para la Pascua Florida;	Tell him that it's me he'll see
darle he yo este mi cuerpo,	about the time of Easter.
el mas lindo que hay en Castilla,	This body will I give to him
si no es él di mi hermana	the loveliest of all Castile,
que de fuego sea ardida;	unless it be my sister dear
y si de mis mas quisiere	may she in Hell be burned.
yo mucho mas le daria;	And if it's more of me he wants
darle he siete castillos	much more will I give him.
los mejores que hay en Castilla.	I shall give him seven castles
	the best in all Castile-land."

Because the origin of these chivalric ballads is shrouded in mystery, the differences in the treatment of them are what interest us most. First the setting: in the Amsterdam version the poem is set in Castile, where an allusion is made to the setting of another famous Spanish ballad, "Fonte frida" ("The Cold Fountain"). However, in the London version, the setting is Hungary, an exotic setting for a Spanish ballad, and the kind of place only mentioned in romances of chivalry or sentimental novels, such as Juan Rodríguez's *Siervo libre de amor*, in which the latter spoke of "Aquel muy alto rrey de Ungria" ("That very lofty king of Hungary").[8] The Amsterdam version hints that the castle with its mention of a gold foundation, merlons of fine silver, and a magic sapphire which glows in the evening is enchanted, but the London version does not. Second, in the London version there is more sentimentality, as Rosaflorida hands her tutor a letter written in blood to be taken to Montesinos. Third, the Rosaflorida in the London version offers Montesinos much more than her Castilian counterpart—thirty as opposed to seven castles, and one hundred gold marks and silk liveries for his servants. Fourth, we have no idea where Montesinos comes from in the London version, but in the Amsterdam version, he is at least presently residing in France. Finally, there is a marked difference in the attitudes of the respective heroines. The Rosaflorida of the Amsterdam version is strong-willed, fiery, and jealous of her sister. She offers herself to her lover, but she shows no weakness in so doing. On the other hand, the Rosaflorida of the London version is virtually irrational in her love for Montesinos, and, as a result, her offerings are extravagant.

Because of the marked differences in the two versions of the ballad, and because of the kinship of the London variant with the works of Juan Rodríguez in its sentimental and novelistic details, it seems safe to say that the variant of the ballad may be attributed to him. As for one critic's assertion that Juan Rodríguez may at best have been a "remaker" rather than the composer *ex nihilo* ("out of nothing"),[9] this contention must be challenged. It has been shown in the light of recent criticism that it is virtually impossible at times to discuss the idea of creation "out of nothing," for that is to suppose no tradition predating a work. Even more difficult would be the case of an individual artist reworking a traditional ballad. If it is to be said at all that Juan Rodríguez is the "remaker" of this ballad, or that the London version of "Rosaflorida" is a mere "remaking," then the "remaking " is so radical as to be declared a separate work of art and should be treated as such. Thus, if Juan Rodríguez is indeed the author of this version, then he is the author and not merely another minstrel slightly modifying a ballad theme. In terms of aesthetics, it has been noted by no less a critic than Ramón Menéndez Pidal himself that the Amsterdam version is more compact and perhaps superior.[10] It is difficult to quarrel with this statement. The version found in the British Museum manuscript is less compact and more sentimental than its counterpart. All that may be said in conclusion, therefore, is that Juan Rodríguez's "Rosaflorida" appears to be the work of an individual author with a nonpopular, strongly aristocratic sensibility.

B *"Conde Arnaldos"* (*"Count Arnaldos"*)

London	London
¡Quien tuviese atal ventura	Would that he such fortune had
con sus amores folgare	as Prince Arnaldos
como el ynfante Arnaldos	with his love
la mañana de San Juane!	all upon Midsummer's Day,
Andando á matar la garça	for the heron did he seek to slay
por rriberas de la mare,	when suddenly upon the shore

vido venir un navio
marinero que dentro viene
dizendo viene esta cantare:
galea, la mi galea,
Dios te me guarde de male,
de los peligros del mundo,
de las ondas de la mare,
del rregolfo de Leone
del puerto de Gibraltare,
que conbaten con la mare.
Oydolo a la prinçesa
en los palaçios do estae:
Si sallesedes, mi madre
sallesedes á mirare:
y veredes como canta
la sirena de la mare.
Que non era la sirena
la sirena de la mare,
que non era sino Arnaldos,
Arnaldos era el ynfante
que por mí muere de amores,
que se queria finare.
¿Quien lo pudiese valera
que tal pena no pagase?

he saw a ship draw near.
Within there was a mariner
who in his ship was singing:
"Galley, my galley,
God keep you from harm,
from the world's many perils,
from the sea's mighty arm;
from the Gulf of Leoné,
and Gibralter's port,
and the castles of Moorish sailors
    three
who strike such terror on the sea."
Within her palace
the princess had heard:
"O come, my mother,
come and see,
mark well the siren of the sea.
But it is not the siren,
the siren of the sea.
It is none other than Arnaldos,
Arnaldos is the prince
who is dying of love for me.
Who would thus his equal be,
who such pain
would not suffer willingly?

Amsterdam

¡Quien hubiese tal ventura
sobre las aguas del mar,
como hubo el conde Arnaldos
la mañana de San Juan!
Con un flacon en la mano
la caza iba cazar,
vió venir una galera
que á tierra quiere llegar.
Las velas traía de seda,
La ejercia de un cendal,
marinero que la manda
diciendo viene un cantar
que la mar facia en calma,
los vientos hace amainar,
los peces andan 'Nel hondo
arriba los hace andar,

Amsterdam

Would that I so lucky could be
upon the waters of the sea
as Arnaldos was that day
all upon Midsummer's Day.
There lay a falcon on his hand
and to the hunt did he stride
when a ship he spied
which did beckon to land.
The sails were all of finest silk,
and the rigging of sheerest gauze,
and the mariner who steered the craft
a song he was singing
which made the waters calm
and all the winds cease blowing.
And the fishes that in the bottom
    swam

las aves que andan volando
en el mástel las face pesar.
Alli fabló el conde Arnaldos,
bien oiréis lo que dirá:
Por Dios te ruego, marinero,
digasme ora ese cantar.
Respondióle el marinero,
tal respuesta la fué a dar:
yo non digo esta cancion
sino á quien conmigo va.

and the birds that in the heavens
  flew
upon the mastheads made their
  home.
Then did speak Arnaldos the Count,
mark well what he did say.
"By God, I pray you, mariner,
tell me forthwith of this song."
The mariner sure did answer him,
such a reply did he him show,
"To no one will I teach this song,
except to him who
with me shall go."

The London version of "Count" or "Prince" Arnaldos is truly, as Menéndez Pidal has stated, a combination or "amalgam" of three ballad themes:[11] Count Arnaldos, Count Niño, and Count Olinos. In the Portuguese version of the Count Niño tale ("O Conde Ninho"), a beautiful princess and her mother are awakened by the magic singing of Count Ninho. When the princess declares her love for the count and her desire to marry him, the mother threatens to have him killed. The daughter replies that if the count is to be slain, she must be slain also. Both lovers are then killed. One is buried at the door of a church and the other at the foot of the altar. From the princess's grave grows a small pine tree and from the count's a tall pine tree. As the trees grow, their ends meet and join together. When the king comes to hear mass, the two pines, symbolic of the lovers, prevent the king from entering the church. When the king orders the trees to be cut, pure milk and "royal blood" ooze out of the trees and then two doves (a small one for the princess and a large one for the count) fly out. When the king sits down at a table, the doves harass him by resting on his shoulder. The ballad ends with the king cursing the love of the princess and the count.

This particular ballad, of the three attributed to Juan Rodríguez, seems nearly incontrovertibly to be his. First, the Amsterdam version describes an enchanted mariner whose ship and manner recall the Flying Dutchman theme.[12] In this version, the time of year is very significant, since it is midsummer, the time of year when supernatural events are rife and pre-Christian beliefs surface.[13] The Amsterdam version concerns only the tempting of Arnaldos by the mariner; the listening and/or reading public is left with a mysterious or perhaps truncated conclusion in which we are not sure as to Arnaldos's decision, and if that decision would lead to his certain death or disappearance.

In the London version, the emphasis is threefold: on Arnaldos, on the mariner, and on the princess. The mariner here does appear to be enchanted, but the princess mistakes him for her lover, Arnaldos, whom she feels is dying of love for her. This is the typical chivalric-sentimental theme of the *Toteslied* or deathsong. Again, as to Juan Rodríguez's being a mere "remaker," we must counter that a "remaking" so drastic as to create a completely new ballad bearing little resemblance to a "traditional" ballad which may or may not have preceded it chronologically,[14] must, in our view, be considered a work of art composed by an individual artist who is, so to speak, writing a variation on a theme. The confusing of Arnaldos with the enchanted mariner is a typical manifestation of the kind of magic transformation which we have already described in such poems as, "Grr, Grr, Flee, For I Rage," and which will reappear in a more pronounced form in his prose works, *Siervo libre de amor* and *Triunfo de las donas*. In addition, the final emphasis is on Arnaldos as a martyr for love, for the princess claims that no one is as worthy as one who would die of love for her. The ending of this ballad bears a great similarity to the final section of *Siervo libre de amor,* in which the narrator is standing on the shore when he is greeted by an enchanted ship manned by maidens dressed in black and captained by an old woman, Synderesis. As in *Conde Arnaldos,* the final section of *Siervo libre de amor* also ends mysteriously.

C *"La hija del rey de Francia"* (*"The Daughter of the King of France"*)

London   London

Yo me iba para Françia   Thus to France did I make my way
do padre y madre tenia;   wherein my parents did stay
errado abia el camino,   but from the road I did stray

errada abia la via;
arryméme á un castillo
por atender compañia.
Por y viene un escudero,
llebesme en tu compañía.
Plázeme, dijo señora,
sí faré por cortesia,
y á las ancas de un caballo
él tomado la abia.
Allá en los Montes Claros
de amores la rrequeria.
Tate, tate (el) escudero
no fagays descortesía:
fija soy de un malato,
y sí bos á mi llegadas
luego sesvos pegaria.
Andando jornadas çiertas
á Francia llegado abia.
Alli fabló la doncella,
bien oyres lo que diria.
es cobarde el escudero
bien lleno de cobardia
tuvo la niña en sus braços
y (el) no supo servilla.

from the path I lost my way.
And to a castle came I
to await some company.
By the road there came a squire:
"Take me in your company."
"Well does it please me, my lady fair,
and I shall do it out of courtesy."
Upon the horse's back
he placed her,
and there in the Clear Mountains
did he woo her.
"Just a minute, squire bold,
do not show discourtesy,
for I the daughter of a leper be,
who is filled with leprosy,
and if you try and come to me,
it will cost you dearly."
After a journey of several days
to France they did arrive.
It was here the damsel spoke,
mark well what she did say.
"The squire is a coward by name
and his cowardice shall be his shame,
for he held the maiden in his arms
and knew not how to serve her."

Amsterdam

De Francia partío la niña;
de Francia la bien guarnida:
íbase para París,
do padre y madre tenia.
Errado lleva el camino,
errado lleva la guia:
arrimarse á un roble
por esperar compañia.
Vio venir un caballero,
que a París lleva la guia.
La niña desque lo vido
le esta suerte le decia:
Si te place, caballero,
lévesme en tu compañia.
Plázeme, dijo, señora,
plázeme, dijo, mi vida.
Apeóse del caballo

Amsterdam

To France did the maiden go
to France so hale and hearty.
to Paris did she make her way
yet did she ever stray.
Upon an oak tree she reclined
to wait for those who would her
guide.
Then did she a knight espy
who to Paris made his way.
And when the maiden did him see
did in this manner say:
"If it please you, gentle knight,
take me in your company."
"Well does it please me, my lady fair,
well does it please me, my life and
soul."
So did the knight

por hacelle cortesía;
puso la niña en las ancas
y él subierase en la silla.
En el medio del camino
de amores la requería.
La niña desque lo oyera
díjole con osadía:
Tate, tate, caballero,
no hagáis tal villanía:
hija soy de un malato

y de una malatía
el hombe que á mi llegase
malato se tornaria.
El caballero con temor
palabra no respondia.
A la entrada de París
la niña se sonreia.
¿De qué vos reis, señora?
¿de qué vos reis, mi vida?
Ríome del caballero,
y de su gran cobardía,
¡tener la niña en el campo,
y catarle cortesía!
Caballero con vergüenza
estas palabras decia:
Vuelta, vuelta, mi señora,
que una cosa se me olvida.
La niña como discreta
dijo: Yo no volveria,
ni persona, aunque volviese,
en mi cuerpo tocaria:
hija soy del rey de Francia
y de la reina Constantina
el hombre que á mí llegase
muy caro le costaria.

from his mount descend
to show his lady courtesy,
and put the damsel in the back
and in the saddle did he ride.
Amorously
in the middle of the road
did he woo her.
When the damsel this did hear
responded in a manner haughty:
"Careful, careful, gentle knight,
do not act so basely,
for my father a leper be
and so strong is his infirmity
that whosoever touches me
shall be afflicted with leprosy."
The gentle knight became afraid
and not a word did say.
At the gates of Paris
the maiden smiled.
"Why smile you so, my lady,
why smile you so, my very soul?"
"I laugh at the gentle knight
and of his cowardly nature,
for he had the maiden in the field
and revered her social station."
The knight did all ashamèd grow
and these words answered thusly:
"Return, return, my lady fair,
for there was one thing I did forget.'
The maiden, for she was all discreet
    did say:
"I never would go back you know,
nor will any soul, though he return
my body bring dishonor,
for I am the daughter of the King
    of France
and of Constantina his consort.
The one who dares my body ap-
    proach
most dearly shall it cost him."

This ballad is the most difficult of the three to assign to Juan
Rodríguez because, unlike the other two, there is no mention

of a lady dying of love for her knight, but rather it is the tale of a maiden testing a knight's courage. Despite small differences in detail, the two ballad versions essentially deal with chivalric as opposed to courtly love, naturalistic as opposed to refined or spiritual love. In contrast with courtly love, chivalric love was the love practiced by the upper nobility and the qualities displayed were those of the conqueror or the superior. In any encounter with members of the lower classes (including the lower nobility), the latter were expected to yield and then be recompensed, either by the love act alone or by some payment of favor. Courtly love and the courtly virtues, with emphasis on restraint and spirituality, were, as in this ballad, objects of scorn. If Juan Rodríguez was the author of this version of "The Daughter of the King of France," it may have been because the work appealed to his sense of class consciousness, for he was a representative of a class whose ethic (courtly love) was not respected by the women of the Castilian aristocracy.

II *"Ardan mis dulçes membranças"* ## (*"May My Sweet Memories Burn"*)

This poem, which appeared in the anonymous *Vida del trovador Juan Rodríguez del Padrón* published by Pedro José Pidal,[15] and in another manuscript,[16] both versions in truncated form,[17] was discovered in a longer, but still as yet incomplete version by Hugo Rennert[18] in the same manuscript in the British Museum in which he found the three chivalric ballads. In its more complete form, the poem is a strongly worded *despedida* or poem of farewell, with the impression that the poet's departure is forced upon him. The first two *serventesios* (double strophes of four octosyllabic lines, each with rhyme scheme *abab*) find the poet echoing one of the most famous insights of Dante:

Ardan mis dulçes membranças	May my sweet memories burn
como yo ardo por ellas	as I burn for them.
pues perdi las esperanzas,	Since I lost all hope
pierdase el plazer con ellas.	let the pleasure perish with them,
Porque no queda con quien	because it is not fitting
parte solo triste y tal	for one who departs so sadly
cordarse de su bien	to remember his happiness
en el tiempo de su mal.	in the time of his misfortune.

These lines appear to paraphrase Dante's "Nessun maggior dolore / che ricordarse del tempo felice / nella misera..." ("No greater sorrow than to remember happy times in one's misery").[19]

Throughout the poem, the poet protests that his service has been in vain and seeks to attain in death what he could not attain in life—happiness:

pues que todo por entero	Since entirely everything
lo que busco y lo que quiero	that I seek and desire
quiça terna la muerte.	perhaps will be had by death.
por ver si terná la muerte	to see if death will have
lo que biviendo no hallo....	what in living I do not find....

The courtly lover, when finding himself in a state of disfavor, is wont to resort to irrational and often bizarre behavior, imitative of the religious ecstacies of the mystics:

¿Mas quien vive asosegado	But who lives calmly
sino aquel qu' es bien querido?	except the one who is well loved?
aquel que vive engañado	He who lives deceived
y anda loco transportado	and walks like a madman
entre las gentes perdido;	lost among the people
como yo quien tu deshaçes	like myself whom you undo
so color de bien hablarme....	under the pretense of speaking kindly to me....

When the lover is well loved (*bien querido*), he walks about in a state of grace, but when he is out of favor, he is in a state of turmoil tantamount to a lover's purgatory.

In his fury, he lashes out at his lady for exiling him:

Porque toda mi alegria	Since all my happiness
se perdió quando party	was lost when I departed
del lugar do te dezia,	from the place I spoke to you about
O dama y señora mia,	O, my lady,
á do me enbias sin mí?	where do you send me without my self?
aquellas partes estrañas,	To those strange lands
donde mi bien se convierte	where my happiness becomes transformed
en pensar como tus mañas,	by thinking how your deceit,
entradas en mis entrañas,	penetrating my feelings,
hazen mi pena tan fuerte.	makes my pain so intense.

The difference between "May My Sweet Memories Burn" and the rest of Juan Rodríguez's production is that the poem does not carefully formulate a reward system for the poet, nor does it plot a lineage for him based on his connection with Macías. Instead, he is simply willing to see if Heaven has more to offer: "que se halle en parayso / lo que la vida no tiene" ("let there be in paradise / what life does not offer").

III *"O desuelada, sandia"* (*"O, Attentive, Foolish Woman"*)

It is with great trepidation that we approach this final poem, even though there is virtually no doubt that it is the work of Juan Rodríguez. What is problematic, however, is that there are three variants of the poem and each variant can alter the meaning of the poem substantially. Because of the reading of one word,[20] it is possible to interpret this poem either as the lament of a lover waiting for his lady who failed to meet him at the appointed rendezvous, or as the complaint of a scorned lady. Because both interpretations are indeed possible, and because we feel obliged to select one, we have chosen to consider the poem as the lament of a woman:

O desuelada, sandia,
loca muger que atendi,
decias: Verne a ty,
e partiste; por tal uia,
deseo sea tu guia.

Por pena, quando fablares
jamas ninguno te crea;
quantos caminos fallares
te bueluan a Basilea.
Vayan en tu compannia
coytas, dolor et cuydados;
fuyan de ti los poblados,
repose et alegria,
claridat et luz del dia.

El troton que caualgares
quede en el primer village;
os puentes por do passares

O, attentive, foolish woman,
insane were you for waiting in vain;
you used to say, "I shall come to you,"
and you departed. Therefore let
your passion be your guide.

For your penance, whenever you speak
may no one ever believe you;
may all the roads you come upon
return you to Basle.
May anguish, pain and care
be your companions.
May well peopled areas flee from you
as well as rest and happiness,
brightness and the light of day.

May the steed you ride
remain in the first village;
may the bridges you cross

quiebren contigo al passaje.
E por mas lealtad mia,
penes, non deuas morir;
si otra cuyadas seruir,
a la hora yo querria
ver la tu postrimeria.
	break as soon as you go over them.
	And, as the result of my loyalty,
	may you not die, but continue to
	   suffer,
	and if you ever intend to serve an-
	   other,
	I will want to see at that time
	your last hour.

En tiempo de los calores fuyan te sombras et rios, ayres, aguas et frescores. Tristaza et malenconia, sean todos tus maniares fasta que aqui tornares delante mi señoria, cridando: ¡Merced! ¡Ualia!	In time of heat may shade and rivers, cool breezes and brooks flee you. May sadness and melancholy be your sustenance until you return here acknowledging my suzerainty and cry "Mercy! She was of great worth!"

"O, Attentive, Foolish Woman" may rightfully be considered a dramatic, impassioned soliloquy, the embryo of a future novel. Touches of a great heroine's lament were already visible in "Rosaflorida" and "Conde Arnaldos," and will reach their culmination in Juan Rodríguez's prose. A biographical note appears with the mention of the Conciliar city of Basle, which apparently must have held an unhappy experience for the author. There is perhaps no one convincing argument for claiming that the poem represents invectives hurled by a female rather than a male, except to say that it would have been most unusual in Juan Rodriguez's era for a male of presumed personal inferiority to heap curses upon any woman, but especially one socially superior, in this fashion.[21] Another point is that it would also have been most unusual for a social inferior to seek a position of superiority ("suzerainty") in the feudalized courtly love relationship. We can only conclude by pointing out that passion of this intensity in a poem of courtly love was also a rare phenomenon and, for twentieth-century taste, greatly to be appreciated.

IV Conclusion

The early fifteenth century in Spain, the era of the reign of John II, is marked by the typical Spanish habit of accepting while at the same time severely modifying, the norms of a literary import, in this case, courtly love. The basic premise of the courtly love movement, the glorification of woman and the deriving of all "worth," spiritual and physical, from her, was at war with the Spanish sense of male superiority and honor. For this reason, courtly love, the love of a social inferior for a lady superior to him, was incompatible with chivalric love, the love of the barons for women of equal or lower station, where the only desired end was physical lovemaking, and only the male's physical prowess, not his spiritual devotion, was appreciated. The poetry of Juan Rodríguez exhibits this clash as poem after poem dwells upon the poet's insistence that he is fully cognizant of the laws of courtly love and that he is complying with the "letter" of the law. Nonetheless, there is a violation of the spirit of the law, for he cannot acknowledge, unlike the majority of his contemporaries, that his lady is in fact superior.

Juan Rodríguez's poetry is both typical and atypical of the poetry of his time: typical in that he uses the standard devices of ecclesiastical parody and casuistry to show that he has complied with the canons of the "religion of love," but atypical in that his martyrdom takes such unconventional forms, revealing his Galician sensibility and his strong attachment to his illustrious predecessor, Macías. Poem after poem alludes to the latter until we are left with the distinct impression that Juan Rodríguez, either seriously or jokingly, considered himself the prototypical martyr for love, either predestined, prefigured, or whatever by Macías. In a series of works, we have seen Juan Rodríguez represent himself as Christ (or St. Francis), Moses, and a werewolf (or howling dog) of love, and each of these personae is meant to convey several impressions: that the force of the "lover's passion" (every pun intended) was indeed great; that the lady in question must have been of the highest nobility; that the lady possesses some form of evil "magic" which leads her lover to his doom, and that because of this magic reason alone is not sufficient to overcome its effects. Although the evidence is scanty, a Celtic influence appears to be present, both in terms of the reincarnation of the hero, and the *geiss* or tragic quest which the hero is forced to undergo because a lady of superior social status forces him into it against his will.

Throughout his poetry there runs a strain of resentment against the Castilian court and courtly norms. In the world of the court, it is commonplace for women of superior social status to govern the amatory lives of courtiers and for love to be a series of empty formalities. When the ambience is solely that of the court, the author assumes a series of poses ranging from *agnus dei* to howling dog, and madness or martyrdom is the only means of escape. When the setting is no longer the court, then the protagonists assume a more equal relationship to each other. Pantasilea, for example, is the equal of Hector, as a warrior, noble, and lover. Such equality of the sexes will be paralleled by the protagonists in the interpolated novel in *Siervo libre de amor*, "Estoria de dos amadores" ("The Story of Two Lovers"). In a similar fashion, poems such as "O desuelada, sandia," and "Rosaflorida," which both take place out of the court, find the heroines to be women of flesh and blood, and in every way on an equal footing with the men.

As is characteristic of the era, the poetry of Juan Rodríguez is uneven in quality, occasionally stereotyped, and when successful, startling, intricate and, at best, suggestive of *tours de force*. Part of the difficulty lies in the very nature of courtly love poetry itself, with its tradition of secrecy and veiled allusions to incidents in the love relationship and the lady's identity. So far we are unable to identify Rodríguez's lady, who may or may not have been Queen María, wife of John II. We can only say for certain that the poet was banished, the court was aware of it, and Rodriguez exploited this bit of misfortune to yield a handsome literary profit.

For formalist critics, the intertwining of the poet's life with his works is an error. Nevertheless, Hispanic criticism and courtly love poetry can only with great difficulty separate the literary personae of Juan Rodríguez from the life of the "Galician troubadour" of the early fifteenth century. For us, Juan Rodríguez must be understood as a man of his era, deeply aware of his people's need for a messianic figure to lead them to complete the reconquest of the Iberian Peninsula, and begin the conquest of Europe and America. As a result, he declares himself courtly love's messiah, for as with the other ruling medieval establishments—the Church, the monarchy and the nobility—no one strong leader emerged to produce stability. On the other hand, because he was a man of his era also, Juan Rodríguez was deeply sensitive about being a minor noble from a part of the peninsula considered inferior to Castile—Galicia. He reacted by flaunting his Galician identity and his knowledge of chivalric and folk culture. Finally, and this is another mark of the era, he was aware (as must be deduced from a knowledge of the era) that the traditional nobility was threatened by the emerging class of converted Jews, and so he clung to his traditional values and attempted to forge a "lineage" for himself by linking his name with the greatest of lovers before him and a true Christian, Macías.

The poetry of Juan Rodríguez reveals as much about the early fifteenth-century social, political, and theological situation as it does about the state of courtly love. Juan Rodríguez's assumption of the role of high priest revealing the God of love's "truth" to the masses of the faithful represents a usurpation of authority, possible only in an era of almost complete anarchy—preimperial, pre-Renaissance, and, above all, premessianic Spain—when all were groping for power and any one could claim it even if no one could hold it for very long. It must be noted by way of conclusion, however, that all of Juan Rodríguez's authority derived not from himself, but, ironically, from that very thing he resented—the social superiority of his lady.

While many critics since the time of María Rosa Lida de Malkiel's monumental study of Juan de Mena[22] have adopted her use of the term "pre-Renaissance" to describe the early fifteenth century in Spain, it has seemed obvious that the literature of this period could equally well be called "manneristic."[23] The poetry of Juan Rodríguez relies heavily upon parodying of social, literary, and ecclesiastical conventions, because he found them empty formalities but had no alternative systems with which to replace them. As with the manneristic period of the late sixteenth century in Spain and Western Europe, failure to find comfort in the established institutions led to a kind of mysticism in which men and women took power—spiritual as well as temporal—into their own hands, and proclaimed themselves possessors of truth and bearers of the word. In such eras, Promethean figures walked the earth, and it is not surprising that in the fifteenth century, offering Joan of Arc and lesser instances of mystic exaltation, Juan Rodríguez should claim for himself the mantle of "greatest of the lovers," both in life and in death. While his martyrdom and subsequent canonization were being proclaimed in lyric poetry, his ultimate glory was to be reserved for the greater possibilities which lengthy narratives such as *Siervo libre de amor* (*The Emancipated Slave of Love*) could offer.

CHAPTER 6

The Emancipated Slave of Love

I *Introduction*

IN the early fifteenth century in Spain, prose was a highly
fluid genre, undergoing many changes in form and content.
Authors of this period generally accepted the classical dictum
that prose was inferior to poetry because it lacked those elements which made poetry superior—meter, rhyme, and meta-
phor; but they were not so willing to be bound by the traditions of Scholasticism, with its host of rules governing the form
of a prose treatise[1] and its belief that all truth was to be
found in the writings of the "authorities"—Aristotle, the Bible,
the Church Fathers, St. Thomas, et al. Because of the experimental nature of the era, the resultant art form was one of
juxtaposition in which an author would work within the confines of the Scholastic treatise, perhaps modifying it to some
degree, and then proceed to show how his personal experience
differed or coincided with the writings of the "authorities."[2]

As we saw in the previous chapter, "truth" meant the "law" of
courtly love, with its basic premise that the lover would be
elevated spiritually by pledging himself to serve his lady self-
lessly, so that he might at least attain spiritual if not social
equality. Many Spanish poets, however, including Juan Rodríguez, were unable to accept this basic premise, but they
worked within the confines of the courtly love code, placing
emphasis upon their own struggles and suffering in order to
prove their "worth." In the case of Juan Rodríguez, mere equal-
ty was not enough. Either because of his Celtic heritage or his
era's fervent desire for a messianic figure, he depicted himself
as a "martyr for love," in part to show that he was the lover
of a very important lady of the upper nobility. What was only

91

hinted at in his poetry—his desire for equality, his fusion of chivalric and courtly love, his Galician nationalism, and his disaffection with the Castilian court—would be given concrete, graphic, and imaginative expression in his sentimental novel, *Siervo libre de amor.*

Closely related to courtly love were the two issues that most concerned Spaniards of the fifteenth century: the equality of women and the definition of true nobility. In his two treatises, *Triunfo de las donas* and *Cadira del honor,* Juan Rodríguez (perhaps largely as a form of flattery), supports the equality of women, but argues against any change in the traditional definition of nobility based on land and lineage. The very treatment of these topics illustrates that the role both of women and of the nobility was changing, and that the traditional medieval hierarchies were being threatened.[3] Juan Rodríguez's other prose works, the *Bursario* (*Pocket-Novel*) and *Epístolas de Ovidio* (*Epistles of Ovid*), a rather faulty translation of Ovid's *Heroides* with an interpolated section, show that the classical texts were not sacred for the writers of this era. Juan Rodríguez was attracted by the sentimental quality of Ovid's work, but he was not above tampering with the text when it offended him or when he felt it could be enhanced by a small addition. In all, the prose of this era was groping to find its own identity and uniqueness. It worked with established models such as the Scholastic treatise of the classical epistle, but it molded them to express its own vision of contemporary reality.

II *An Autobiographical Journey*

Unquestionably, *The Emancipated Slave of Love* (*Siervo libre de amor*) is Juan Rodríguez's best-known work even though it is likely a fragment, for the third and final section is apparently incomplete. Like most of his poetry, the work is more or less autobiographical in that it deals with his ill-fated love for a lady of the upper nobility. All of the traits peculiar to Juan Rodríguez are found here—preoccupation with his own personal suffering, unwillingness to accept a subordinate role in the courtly love relationship, and the desire for immortality as a martyr for love. Also present to a more marked degree than in his poetry is a preoccupation with Galician folklore and Celtic myth, consciously manipulated to enhance his prestige as a martyr for love by once more associating his name with Macías's and, ultimately (although the evidence is not on the firmest of grounds) linking his destiny with King Arthur's.

As the creator of the sentimental novel in Spain, Juan Rodríguez began his work in the manner of a typical Scholastic treatise,[4] dividing the story of his love affair into three stages: when he was in love and his love was requited; when he was in love but his lady no longer loved him; and, finally, when he was no longer in love nor was he loved but was irrevocably changed by love's power. Each stage is presented allegorically as a journey and has a path symbolized by a tree and one of the human faculties: the first stage, "De Bien Amar y Ser Amado" ("Loving Well and Being Loved") is "the road of the green myrtle (*verde arrayan*) planted in the spacious path which is called "loving well" and is symbolized by the heart; the second is the road of the poplar tree or tree of paradise, "planted in the descending path which is called desperation" and is symbolized by the free will; and the third path is symbolized by "the green olive, planted in the very bitter and narrow path" followed by the "enslaved reason."

The work begins as the author explains that his work is autobiographical and narrates a more or less realistic account of his unhappy love affair in which he gives tantalizing hints about the lady's identity and how he lost her favor: "yo aver sydo bien affortunado, avnque agora me vees en contrallo; e por amar, alcanzar lo que mayores de mi deseavan...." ("It was quite fortunate, although you now see me in the opposite condition; and because of love, I attained what those superior to me desired....") He explains how his lady cast her eyes upon him, but at first he could not believe his good fortune: "Sy algun pensamiento a creer me lo induzia, yo de mi corria, y menos savio me juzgava...." "... quanto mas della me veya acatado, mas me tenia por despreciado...." ("If some thought induced me to believe it, I fled from myself and thought myself less wise...." "... the more I saw myself noticed by her, the more I felt myself being despised....") As he begins to fall in love, he is warned by Discretion that he is yielding his free will to

Love, a god whom in the past the author had scorned in verse, and now Love will have his revenge. As the love between the author and the lady grows, the former chooses a confidant, "a discreet friend" (*amigo discreto*), who later turns out to be a typical *lisongier* or flatterer, whose treachery causes the lady to turn against him and which ultimately leads to his banishment.

The friend advises the author to send his lady a letter, confessing his love, and, taking the friend's advice, he sends her the following:

Recebyd alegre mente,	Receive joyfully,
mi señora, por estrenas	my lady, as a first token,
la presente.	this letter.
La presente cançion mia	This my first song
vos embia	offers you,
en vuestro logar despaña,	in your land of Spain,
a vos y a vuestra conpaña,	to you and all your retinue,
alegria;	happiness:
e por mas ser obediente,	and, even more obediently,
mi coraçon en cadenas	my heart in chains,
por presente.	for the moment.
E pues yo hize largueza	And since I was so generous,
syn promesa de los bienes	without promising those goods
que poseya,	which I possessed,
plega a vuestra señoria	may your ladyship
en tal dia	at the proper moment
estrenar vuestro siruiente,	grant your servant an interview
librandole de las penas	and free him of the pains
que oy syente.	which he now suffers.

And at long last, the lady responds and offers him the private interview: ". . . el punto una hora, la hora un dia, el dia un año me pareçia, hasta venir aquel ledo mensaje por el qual me fue prometido logar a la fabla e merçed al seruiçio." (". . . a second seemed an hour, an hour a day, a day a year, until that happy message which granted me a place to speak to her and thanked me for my service.")

In the meantime, however, the traitorous friend, feigning friendship all the while, worked behind his back to alienate the lady, and finally he succeeded: "El menos fiable, que es desleal amigo, avnque fengia todo el contrario, trabajando venir; yo no sabidor, por destierro de mi impunançia de aquella..., donde fue contra mi indignada la muy exçelente señora de mi, no me atreguando la vida...." ("The least trustworthy of all, the disloyal friend, even though he feigned the opposite, sought to attain, unbeknownst to me, her favor, by turning her against me.... Whereby my most excellent lady became indignant with me and did not grant me a minute's peace....")

Part 1 is a mixture of medieval allegory with some hint of techniques presaging the Renaissance. While the first section does present a love story that is a typical tale of a troubadour and his lady, there is a very pointed reference to the lady's having initiated the love affair and to the author's inability to handle court intrigue. There is a strong sense in this first part that earthly love, symbolized by the goddess Venus and the green myrtle, the time of the author's good fortune and a time never to be regained, is something which does not fit neatly into Scholastic categories or classical mythology.

In the second section, the "Solitary and Dolorous Contemplation" ("Solitaria e Dolorosa Contemplaçion"), the author begins an allegorical journey "... through the jungle of my thoughts" ("... por la selva de mis pensamientos") and arrives at the crossroads of the three paths of loving. With his arrival at the first path ("Loving Well and Being Loved"), the green myrtle dedicated to the goddess Venus loses its greenery; the tree symbolizing the third path, the green olive dedicated to the goddess of wisdom, Minerva, does likewise, and the birds lose their song. Thus, under the sway of the free will, he enters the second path, symbolized by the poplar tree or tree of paradise, dedicated to Hercules,[5] descending to find the Elysian Fields ("Campos Yliasos"), guided by "Understanding."

As he begins his journey, Understanding warns him that he dares to enter the "house of Pluto" ("casa de Pluton") and that he is sure that "... antes del quarto cerco donde penan los que mueren por bien amar, te sera vedado el paso" ("... before the fourth circle where those who died for love suffer, you will be prohibited from entering"), and therefore he will not attain the ninth and final circle. The author, in desperation, curses death and before expiring wishes that death would grant him what it granted to Ardanlier, son of King Creos of Mondoya and his consort, Senesta.

Part 2 represents Juan Rodríguez's attempt to display his knowledge of classical mythology. As the author, guided by Understanding, wanders through the classical underworld meeting a host of figures which include no less than Theseus, Phaedra, Hippolytus, Apollo, Latona, Proserpine, Sisyphus, Tantalus, and many others, the result is little more than a catalog. The effect of this listing is that the second part is artistically weak, so weak in fact that this classical solution proves no solution at all. Thus, the author is forced to seek his answer both out of the court and away from those techniques traditionally associated with the court; namely, allegory and mythology, and to turn instead to the field, where folklore and enchantment have free reign.

There then follows the most famous part of the work, "The Story of Two Lovers" ("Estoria de dos amadores"). This part of the novel is, strictly speaking, the second half of the second section, but because it is neither a realistic narrative nor yet an allegory but rather a sentimental-chivalric tale, it has life of its own, and might be considered a third part. Here we are transported to the realm of chivalric fantasy to meet Ardanlier, the young prince who flees with his love, Liessa, because both families are against the match. In his journey with Liessa, Ardanlier achieves great fame because of his extraordinary beauty and prowess in the lists. When he arrives at the French court, the Princess Yrena falls in love with him, but knowing that he is pledged to Liessa, offers herself to him in the following manner: "... en señal de buen amar, mando obrar vn sotil candado de fyno or, poblado de vertuosas piedras que no recebian estyman; ... e que promessa hazia alto Cupido, hijo de de la deesa, ... nunca jamas torcar la invencion; ni soltar dela figurada prisyon su catyuo coraçon, hasta que al señor delas llaues plugiese abrir y librar dela pena ala padeciente Yrena." ("... as a token of her true love, she ordered a handcuff of fine gold made, encrusted with magic stones whose value was inestimable; ... and she promised lofty Cupido, son of the goddess, never to change the combination, nor to free her captive heart from the adorned prison, until it pleased the keeper of the keys to open it and free the suffering Irene from pain." Leaving the French court, the couple travels to Central and Eastern Europe where Ardanlier wins great fame by aiding the Holy Roman Emperor, Albert II of Germany, to dislodge King Wladislaw of Poland from Bohemia. At last they come to Spain, to the city of Venera (Padrón, the author's birthplace), where they have built for themselves a subterranean palace: "... e muy sotiles geometricos que por marauillosa arte rrompieron una esquiua rroca, e dentro dela qual obraron vn siecreto palaçio, rrico y fuerte, bien obrado." ("... and very subtle geometrists, who, by marvelous arts, broke a stubborn rock and inside of it built a secret palace, rich and well made.")

After seven years have passed, Ardanlier's father, King Creos himself, sets out to find his son and comes to the city of Venera. There he finds Ardanlier's three hunting dogs and follows them. The dogs lead him to Liessa and when Creos comes upon her, he accuses her of stealing his only son and in a furious rage, draws his sword and kills both Liessa and her unborn baby. After the terrible act, Lamidoras, the trusted tutor of Ardanlier, discovers his lady dead and when Ardanlier happens along later, he accuses his tutor of murder. Lamidoras, with utmost grief and desperation, tells his master what really happened. Ardanlier then orders Lamidoras to follow his instructions. With his own blood as ink, he writes a letter to Yrena and gives her the key to the handcuff, so that she may now be released from her amorous bondage. After writing the letter, Ardanlier picks up his sword and kills himself, joining his beloved Liessa in death.

Lamidoras travels to France and presents the Princess with the key and the epistle. After hearing the tragic news, the princess takes an oath that she will make a pilgrimage to the sepulchre of Ardanlier and Liessa, construct a temple in their honor on the site, and in the company of virgins, pray for the redemption of their souls. After a difficult sea voyage, the princess and her retinue arrive at Venera. Descending to the underground palace, the Princess orders "... that two sepulchres be constructed of four magic stones," upon which she places the following epitaph: "In deepest grief, may the cruel death of the most loyal Ardanlier and Liessa, who died for love, be an

example and perpetual memory for you, o lovers. . . ." And
upon the tombs are carved the images of four stone lions who
will one day come to life.

This mysterious inscription is not deciphered until after the
respective deaths of Lamidoras and Yrena. Upon the death of
the latter, the underground palace becomes enchanted and no
one is able to penetrate the three chambers—the first, the tomb
of Lamidoras, the second, the tomb of Yrena, and the third,
that of the two lovers—unless he be ". . . a conqueror and a
loyal lover." Many great knights and princes attempt the quest,
coming from far away to take up residence outside the enchanted, underground palace, but none are successful until the
arrival of the knight Macías, ". . . born at the foot of that harsh
mountain. . . ." Macías, by his courage, virtue and loyalty as a
lover, penetrates the first, second, and finally the third chamber.
With the quest over, the knights who took up residence in Venera
are permitted to enter the enchanted tombs five times a year:
May Day (the anniversary of the lovers' death), and the twenty-
fourth and twenty-fifth of June and July, days on which Cupid
pardons all lovers their sins.[6] On these days, magical things
happen: the respective mounts of Ardanlier and Liessa become
wild, seeking refuge in the forest (a whole race of wild horses
descending from them), and a race of wild dogs evolves from
the hunting dogs of Ardanlier. Others say, however, that the
thirteen dogs of Ardanlier remained at the tomb and were
turned to stone. So strong was their loyalty that they chose
to stay there until the Day of Judgment. The story ends with
the author claiming that he himself is descended from Macías:
"And all those who descended from him [Macías], of whom I
am the least, rich in the name of being of the virtuous, and
sole inheritor of his loyalty."

The fourth and final section of *The Emancipated Servant of
Love* bears no heading, although, as was mentioned above, it
relates the period of the author's life when he neither loved nor
was loved. In this final section, he turns away from the precipi-
tous path of free will and follows the more difficult and narrow third road, the path of Minerva, goddess of wisdom, symbolized by the green olive tree. In this final state, wherein the
author recovers his equilibrium, he begins by reciting two

poems showing his present state to be one of a realization of the effects of love. The first poem, which we shall reproduce below, is an awareness that the lover may no longer be *in* love, but that if he is a true lover, he is never free from the effects of love:

Avnque me vedes asy
catyvo, lybre naçy.

Although you see me here
a slave, I was born free.

Catyvo, lybre naçy,
y despues, como sandio,
perdy mi libre aluedrio,
que no so señor de mi.
Syn cobrar lo que perdy,
nin fallar mi poderyo,
¿como dyre que soy mio?

A slave, I was born free
and afterwards, like a fool,
I lost my free will,
and now I no longer am my master.
Without recovering what I lost
or finding my powers,
how shall I say that I am I?

¿Como dire que soy mio,
pues no soy enteramente?
Avnque dyxesse otra mente,
diria vn grand desuario.
Por ende, digo y porfyo
que por servir leal mente,
no soy syeruo, mas syrviente.

How shall I say that I am I,
since I am not myself entirely?
Although I might say otherwise,
I would be saying an untruth.
Therefore I say and insist
that because I served loyally,
I am not a slave, but a servant.

No soy siervo, mas syrviente,
pues que libre fuy llamado
en el tiempo ya passado,
que no puede ser presente,
quando yo primera mente
conoçy, por mi pecado,
la que me tyene oluidado.

I am not a slave but a servant,
since I was called free
in a time now past
which cannot be the present,
when I, because of my sins,
first came to know
the one who has forgotten me.

La que me tyene oluidado
se piensa que padeçer
es el verdadero ser
de qual quier enamorado.
Vereys do syervo, cuytado!
¡O quien se pudiese ver
fuera de estraño poder!

The one who has forgotten me
may think that suffering
is the true state
of any lover.
You will see where I serve, alas!
Would that I could see myself
free of this strange power!

Fuera destraño poder
en el tiempo que solia,
¡quantas vezes maldizia

Free of this strange power,
as I used to be in previous times.
How often did I curse those whom

los que via asy perder,
no pensando de caher,
nin seguir la triste via
de quien tanto mal dizia!

De quien tanto mal dizia,
syendo libre syn cuydado,
¿que dira, syendo forçado
del sentido que avia?
¡Llamays ventura la mia!
Quanto menos soy amado,
damor soy mas aquexado.

Damor soy mas aquexado
que omne de su valia:
ya no se ques alegria,
plazer, ni buen gasajado,
que, par dios, aunque me via,
¿pensays que me conoçia?

¿Pensays que me conoçia?
Par dios, no me conoçi:
tan turbado me senty
del semblante que traya.
E asy dira todavia:
Avnque me vedes asy
catyvo, lybre naçy.

I said did condemn themselves,
not thinking that I too should fall
or follow the sad path
of him who spoke so ill!

Of him who spoke so ill,
being free, without care,
what shall I say, being impelled
by the feelings I had?
Do you call me lucky?
The less I am loved,
the more I am vexed by love!

I am more vexed by love
than a man of such worth:
I no longer know what is happiness,
pleasure or pleasant company.
By God, although I were to gaze
    upon myself,
do you think I would know me?

Do you think I would know me?
By God, I did not recognize myself,
so disturbed
did my countenance appear.
And so do I still continue to say,
although you see me like a slave,
I was born free.

Continuing in a state of anguish, the author comes to the shore of the ocean, where he is greeted by a miraculous sight: a great ship, whose sails and rigging are all in black. The captain of this ship is an old woman dressed in black, and the crew is made up of seven maidens, all in mourning. The old woman, whose name is Synderesis, orders the ship to sail toward the shore and then she enters a small boat to row to shore in order to gather provisions, make repairs, and ready herself for a defense against her enemies. As she lands, she greets the author and asks him about his adventures and he does likewise with her. At this point the work abruptly ends.

It is our belief that the two final sections of *The Emancipated Slave of Love* can only be understood in the light of the author's biography, and the Galician-Celtic influence which permeates his works and those of his forerunners, composers of the romances of chivalry. In terms of structure, the first part of the work, "De Bien amar e Ser Amado" ("Loving Well and Being Loved") is merely a simple narrative of his love affair at the court, an environment he found distasteful because of the intrigue and duplicity there which eventually led to his banishment. The second part of the work, describing the author's descent into an allegorical inferno guided by his understanding, clearly indicates that reason or the understanding alone is insufficient to release the author from his pains, for he is unable to attain the "Campos Yliasos" ("Elysian Fields") or ninth circle of Pluto. By attaining only the fourth, or lover's, circle, the reader is advised that the author's spiritual journey has led him to a kind of lover's purgatory, from which he must eventually be released by other than rational means.[7] Thus, at the end of this section, the author cries out that he wishes his fate to be that of Ardanlier's, for Ardanlier's tale is the first step toward a solution.

"The Story of Two Lovers" is intended to be the second half of the second section, for it is a chivalric-sentimental tale on an imaginative plane which clearly parallels the autobiographical story of Juan Rodríguez and his lady of high social station. However, there are certain important differences, as one critic has mentioned. For instance, Ardanlier and Liessa are both royalty, both of the upper nobility. As opposed to the usual story line of sentimental novels from Italy,[8] there is no adulterous relationship, even though a possible triangle is hinted at when the Princess Yrena pledges herself chastely to Ardanlier, knowing she can never be his. As is customary in sentimental novels, the love relationship can only end unhappily, usually in death, banishment, or both. In this story, both lovers die, and both remain unredeemed, for one was murdered and the other committed suicide. The key to the lovers' redemption is in two parts: the Princess Yrena must prepare the shrine or Holy Grail,[9] and the quest must be undertaken by the purest and worthiest of lovers, Macías. The Arthurian parallels are obvious.

"The Story of Two Lovers" is, as Edward Dudley has noted, a contrast between court and country.[10] In Dudley's article, a

dichotomy is created between Ardanlier's two loves, Liessa and
the Princess Irene, with the former representing his love of
flesh and blood, and thereby symbolizing the country, and the
latter his "idealized" love, symbolizing the court.[11] Such a
dichotomy should not be carried too far, however, for the two
worlds are constantly intermingled. For example, when Ardanlier, son of King Creos de Mondoya, and Liessa, daughter of
the great Lord of Lira, are supposedly fleeing from the malig-
nant atmosphere of the court, the departure is effected with
great pomp and majesty: "Traspuesta la Vrsa menor, mensajera
del alua, caualga su dama de rrienda, bien acompañados de
rricas y valyosas piedras, en gran larguesa del señor delos
metales; e cuya reguarda venia el su fiel ayo Lamidoras, y
Bandyn, esclavo de aquella." ("And when the constellation
Ursa Minor, messenger of the Dawn, disappeared, his lady came
on horseback and the two carried a generous quantity of the
sovereign of the precious metals, and in their retinue were his
loyal tutor, Lamidoras, and Bandyn, her slave.") Following
the elopement, in an obvious reversal of the usual courtly love
pattern, Irene, the princess of France, pledges her love to
Ardanlier in an elaborate ritual in which she becomes *his* slave
by placing her heart in a golden padlock and promising to keep
it there until he releases her. When Ardanlier dies prematurely,
Irene, the alleged symbol of the court and "pure love," makes a
pilgrimage to Venera, to the underground palace, and there
constructs the lovers' tombs. After her own death, the underground palace becomes enchanted and thus the cycle is com-
pleted: the court, in the person of Irene, has come to the country,
but the underground palace can hardly be called "the country"
in the usual sense. It can only be said that all enchantment takes
place in the country and none in the court. Enchantment has
been said to be the means by which the artificiality of the court
is transformed into the earthier aspects of the field. Nonetheless, the supposedly "earthier" aspects of the field are negated
by the elaborate ceremonies and wealth to be found in the underground palace built by the "subtle geometricians," and the
army of knights errant who, after the death of Ardanlier, Liessa,
and Irene, surround the underground sepulchral chambers. By
way of conclusion, it must be observed that all three lovers,

Ardanlier, Liessa, and Irene are buried together—a kind of posthumous *ménage à trois* linking court and country—but Irene remains in another chamber, and only the tombs of Ardanlier and Liessa undergo a magic process which results in the liberation of their souls. All, of course, pay homage to Ardanlier, including Macías, whose magic is reminiscent of the Arthurian figures who preceded him, and especially, Sir Galahad.

But there is another element that has been neglected here. As has been noted by previous critics, the tale of Ardanlier and Liessa does bear certain resemblances to the legend of St. James's arrival in Spain.[12] It is our belief that this is no mere coincidence, for the story of Ardanlier and Liessa was intended to be ecclesiastical parody on a grand scale: Ardanlier is a kind of St. James of the religion of love, thus establishing Spain, and more specifically, Padrón (Venera), birthplace of the author, as the holiest shrine of the courtly love world. Before discussing the parallels, it is necessary to recall the legend of St. James. According to the Calistine Codex,[13] after the Saint's martyrdom in Jerusalem, the body of the apostle, accompanied by his two disciples, Atanasius and Theodorus, arrived miraculously at the shore of what is now Padrón in Spain. The moment they landed, the two disciples placed the body upon a rock and the rock received the body as though it were a sepulchre made for that purpose. When the disciples tried to find a site for burial, they came to the pagan queen, whose name was Lupa,[14] and she directed them to a Roman official who put them in jail. According to legend, they were freed by an angel of the Lord, but were pursued by the Roman official's knights. However, as the latter were pursuing the disciples across the bridge, the bridge collapsed and the knights were drowned. Once more the disciples came to Lupa and she told them they should harness two oxen to a cart and that the cart would take them to the burial site. The oxen were, in reality, two wild bulls, but miraculously, the bulls became tame and led the two disciples right back to the palace of the queen. Convinced now of the divinity of the apostle's sepulchre, the queen accepted Christianity and in the process converted her people. The body was buried and the disciples died soon afterward and were buried on either side of the apostle. For centuries, however, the site of the body was forgotten until discovered by the hermit Pelayo, who informed Archbishop Theodomirus; the latter communicated the news to King Alphonse II, known as "the Chaste." Soon afterward, according to legend, the Saint himself appeared in the battle of Clavijo against the Moors,[15] and from that moment on, Santiago (St. James) became the patron saint of Spain, and his burial site the object of worldwide pilgrimages, competing with Rome for the title of holiest shrine in all of Christendom.[16]

If it is true, as Roger Sherman Loomis has sought to prove, that there is a direct connection between the story of the arrival of Joseph of Arimathea to England and the Arthurian romances of chivalry,[17] then there may be a precedent for the legend of Santiago and the chivalric-sentimental tale of Ardanlier and Liessa. If, according to Loomis, Glastonbury, the site of the death of King Arthur and his supposed "translation" to godhead is also the site of the arrival of the apostle to England, and, further, if there is a direct connection between the Castle of the Holy Grail and the death of the apostle, then there may be assumed a parallel relationship between the death of Ardanlier, the conversion of his sepulchre into a holy shrine, and the events of the arrival, burial, and magic appearance of Santiago in Spain.

Another aspect of Juan Rodríguez's tale may be his era's desire for a messianic figure, for "The Story of Two Lovers" is a nationalistic work on two grounds: Spain becomes the new international capital of courtly love, with its capital city at Venera or Padrón, the holiest shrine of the religion of love. It must be remembered that there is a precedent for all this, because in the Middle Ages, Santiago de Compostela competed directly with Rome for primacy as the holiest of shrines. And the Galician bishop, Diego Gelmírez, considered himself a pope and appointed cardinals.[18] It may be that Juan Rodríguez, spurned by the Castilian court, created a rival center in his home town—an area which spawned not only saints of the Church, but "saints" of the religion of love—Ardanlier, Macías, and, lastly, Juan Rodríguez himself, as we shall soon see.

The end of "The Story of Two Lovers," by which the author establishes himself as of the lineage of Ardanlier and Macías, serves to usher in the final section wherein the author himself will be redeemed. The appearance of the miraculous boat, manned by Synderesis and her crew of seven virgins dressed in black, would appear to have its parallel in the appearance of the Lady of the Lake, who carried Arthur to the land of Avalon.[19] Now that the author is freed of the passions of love (albeit unable to find a rational means for salvation), Synderesis will furnish it for him: apotheosis as a martyr for love. Surely the author will die of love, but, as a result of his loyalty, his fate will be similar to that of his great predecessors, Macías and Ardanlier.

By every criterion, *The Emancipated Slave of Love* is Juan Rodríguez's most ambitious work. It is an artistic experiment and therefore not wholly successful. The second section, "Solitary and Dolorous Contemplation," is the least successful part and the author was wise to abandon the use of an abstruse allegory filled with unsatisfying allusions to Greek mythology. "The Story of Two Lovers," on the other hand, is the most adequately contrived section, partly because it is the most imaginative, and perhaps partly because it is a true expression of Galician nationalism. As is usual with Juan Rodríguez, there is basic questioning of the code of courtly love. For this reason, the work focuses mainly on the male protagonist, Ardanlier, who embodies the finest characteristics of chivalry and courtliness. The female characters are one-sided and symbolize courtly and chivalric love respectively. Liessa is Ardanlier's physical love. He takes her from her parents (in essence, kidnaps her), travels about the world with her, and then she dies with his child in her womb. The only courtly aspect of Ardanlier's relationship with Liessa is his loyalty, for he is equal to her in every way, even socially. Yrena, on the other hand, represents courtly love in reverse. It is she who pledges herself to serve Ardanlier without hope of reward and even travels to his sepulchre, prepares a shrine for him, and holds the key to his eventual redemption.

It is of vital significance, given Juan Rodríguez's era, with its imperial and messianic longings, that Ardanlier be an international traveler and warrior as well as lover, for he will furnish his creator with an impeccable, if wholly imaginative, lineage. When in the final section the author does achieve an implied apotheosis, it is as if he were affirming that his love affair and his suffering merited it for him, as well as his "pure" blood line.

As Dinko Cvitanovič has noted,[20] Juan Rodríguez's sentimental novel is a precursor of the Renaissance in two ways: in its attempt to immortalize the author, and in its elevation of love to a position of psychological significance outside the framework of Christian or classical thought. Cvitanovič points out that the great figures of the Renaissance sought to immortalize themselves in a variety of ways: through their art, through their deeds, or through someone else's art. Thus, it was not uncommon for those of great wealth and position to commission a work bearing their likeness—a bust, a painting, or, the quintessential genre of the Renaissance, a medallion. In a similar fashion, *The Emancipated Slave of Love* is Juan Rodríguez's medallion, his vehicle for obtaining immortality. The first and second parts of *The Emancipated Slate of Love* focus directly on autobiographical elements which demonstrate his worthiness as a courtier and lover; the third and fourth parts focus upon mythical elements which elevate and transform him, for "The Story of Two Lovers" serves to legitimize the author's patrimony by showing his descent from a great line of martyrs for love, while the final section exhibits his Arthurian-like "translation" to godhead.

In a similar fashion, the effects of love upon men and women are no longer limited to the boundaries of either the Church's teachings or to the courtly love code as it was understood in the late Middle Ages. The author, as presented in the first two and fourth sections, and Ardanlier in Part 3, are not merely idealized warriors, courtiers, or lovers. Nor are they merely precursors of future idealized figures in Spanish literature such as Amadís de Gaula.[21] Neither must the sometimes abstruse symbolism and allegorical framework of the first and fourth parts obscure the realism and intensity of love's hold over human beings and their inability to come to terms with it. In the second and third parts, as the author and Ardanlier struggle vainly to overcome love's effects, neither the Christian dichotomy of the spirit and the flesh, nor the courtly love code suffice, for mere mortification of the flesh on the one hand and mere obedience to the lady's will on the other are insufficient to remove the indelible effects of earthly love.

Medieval techniques, such as allegorical symbolism, are employed in this work to present ideas anticipating those of the coming era. The author's descent in the "Circles of Pluto," which symbolizes the lover's dilemma, is an example of exaggerated adherence to an outmoded literary tradition, which had yet to be replaced by a new form of narrative. The late Middle Ages, a stage of transition in both literary technique and thought, permitted artists the freedom to juxtapose such disparate elements as allegory, an interpolated novel, and a mythical voyage. If Juan Rodríguez wished to arrive at inner peace, he could do so by using new and untried means. At this moment in time, his efforts seem to have been at least partially successful.

CHAPTER 7

Minor Prose Works

I Triunfo de las donas (The Triumph of Women)

THE *Triumph of Women* and *Cadira del honor* (*The Seat of Honor*) are probably companion pieces written at the same time and dedicated to Queen María of Aragon, wife of John II. Given the supposed date of the compositions (around 1438),[1] and the fact that *The Triumph of Women* is such a one-sided defense of women, we can only conclude that the author wrote it to ingratiate himself with the Queen in the hope that he would be permitted to return to Spain afer his long exile.

The necessity for a defense of women was occasioned in Spain by the famous (or infamous) Torrellas affair, in which Pedro Torrellas composed a poem which was later to be termed the "Maldezir de mugeres" ("The Cursing of Women"). Torrellas showed women to possess all the vices possible to make them untrustworthy and capable of leading men to unhappiness and perdition.[2] The reaction to this poem caused the various court poets as well as some clergymen to either defend women against these attacks or else to produce new works which defended Torrellas's position and attacked women, although scarcely ever as vehemently as did the antifeminists of other countries.[3]

The arguments against woman have their origins in the Hebrew and Christian interpretations of the role of Eve, the Proverbs of Salomon, St. Paul, Aristotle, St. Jerome, St. Augustine, and Juvenal's Sixth Satire ("Against Women"), as well as a host of medieval writers including Boccaccio[4] and the writers of the lives of the saints. The defenders of woman are nearly as numerous, and the entire cult of courtly love and the romances of chivalry are often a testament to the equality if not the superiority of woman's talent, beauty, and virtue. The most famous antifeminist work of the fifteenth century in

Spain is Alfonso Martínez de Toledo's condemnation of the lasciviousness of women in the *Corbacho,* but even his condemnations are tempered by assigning the burden of guilt to both sexes. Indeed, as more than one feminist advocate has stated, the most vituperative antifeminism is more often to be found in the literature written by converted Jews in Spain rather than by Christians.[5] Proof of this is that the culmination of the antifeminist trend in literature is, without doubt, *La Celestina,* whose author (or authors) was a converted Jew.

To the defense of women sprang many of the most famous court poets and prose writers, such as Gómez Manrique, the Condestable de Portugal, Álvaro de Luna, Fernando de la Torre, Enrique de Villena, Juan de Flores, and Juan Rodríguez. Although the latter's attitude toward woman is often harsh, as a result of his quarrel with the basic tenets of courtly love, in which he refused to accept a subordinate role, nevertheless it must be admitted that in *The Triumph of Women* he offers a most cavalier defense.

The work begins at daybreak with the author in the company of six youths at the Cave of the Basilisk, which no doubt symbolizes the court, to which he was forbidden entrance. There his six young friends ask him who is more noble and virtuous, man or woman? Unable to find an answer, he goes to a "solitary place" surrounded by wild plants and there he comes upon a fountain exuding fresh and clear waters. As the narrator begins to speak ill of women in order to present the arguments both for and against them, the fountain suddenly begins to gush forth tears and a voice is heard. It is the voice of the nymph Cardiana, saddened by the author's harsh words. The author protests and asks to be pardoned, so the voice of the fountain forgives him but speaks ill of the "... cursing and vituperative *Cobarcho* [that is, Boccaccio], offender of the worth of womanhood," and then offers him incontrovertible proof of the superiority of women by means of a long treatise in which fifty reasons are given.

Many of the medieval arguments proferred by feminist authors have become commonplaces and these are found among the fifty given by Cardiana and include the following: Eve, the first woman, was created in Paradise and from human material,

Adam's rib, as opposed to Adam, who was created from the earth in the Valley of Damascus. Another argument adduced, often to prove the equality rather than the superiority of woman, is that Eve was created neither from Adam's head nor his foot but from his middle, wherein is found the most noble part of man, his heart: "The fourth [reason], because she was created from the middle, and not from the extremities of man; since virtue is found in the middle and most noble dwelling of the soul, which is the heart."

Other commonplaces to be found in *The Triumph of Women* are the superiority of woman's beauty and the invocation of the divinity of the Virgin Mary, as well as the virtue of personages from the Bible, Esther and Judith, along with women reknowned in classical legend, such as Penthasileia and Dido. The originality of *The Triumph of Women* lies in some of the ingenious, original proofs such as the fact that women are cleaner because "...as many times after a woman is seen washing herself the water remains clear as it was in the beginning and on the contrary if a man washes himself the water always becomes cloudy, since man was created of the unclear vapor of the earth and woman of clean, purified flesh." The thirteenth reason lays the blame for the Fall at Adam's feet, for Cardiana claims that Eve merely offered Adam the apple which was expressly forbidden to man, and that he did the actual tasting.

Another proof, which contemporary audiences might find amusing, is the fourteenth reason, which finds women less shameful, since a woman's pubic hair covers her genitals completely as compared with man: "...she is more modest, inasmuch as her hair grows to such a point as to cover the more shameful parts...something which nature did not wish to grant to man." Also of contemporary interest is Cardiana's reference to the normal posture of the lovemaking act in which the woman's usual position is that of facing the "...celestial bodies, as befits the property of the rational animal; man beholds the lower things, following the quality of the brutish animals."

In addition to defending woman as superior in chastity and the principal virtues—pity, compassion, fortitude, temperance, and justice—Cardiana invokes an ingenious theological proof:

she claims that the Redeemer took the form of man, because had he taken the form of woman, this would have shown that woman caused the Fall, and therefore it was woman who needed redeeming: "... and the twenty-sixth reason is: because our Redeemer did not take the appearance of woman, but of man; for if He had taken the appearance of woman, it would have seemed that He came to redeem the sin of woman, and that it was she who had condemned us to perpetual suffering." Further proofs concerning the Redeemer are that women were the first to greet Him at the tomb on the day of the resurrection and that it was man who deceived Him, mistreated Him and slew Him.

After a long list of the notable women of three continents, Asia, Africa, and Europe, the nymph Cardiana ends with praise for Spain and for Spain's queen. When the voice of the fountain is still, the author asks her how she was transformed from a woman into a fountain and the voice reveals that she is Cardiana who was beloved by Aliso, who killed himself for love, and who was transformed by the gods into an ash tree, and when she beheld his new form, she was transformed into a fountain. Her last words to the author are to beg him to refresh the roots of the ash tree in order that by so doing the fates will be kinder to him than they were to her. The author follows her instructions and waters the trunk and limbs of the tree and the tree begins to revive and become green with foliage. After completing his errand of mercy, he departs and ends the work by offering it to his lady, the queen.

There is much in *The Triumph of Women* that is commonplace in feminist literature of the fifteenth century in Spain. Nearly all such works offer a list of chaste women in history, the crimes of men, and women who exemplify the principal virtues. There are also attempts to refute Salomon, Aristotle, Paul, Augustine, and, principally, Boccaccio. Juan Rodríguez's originality lies in presenting arguments which strike an ingenious and contemporary note; arguments which deal with human sexuality and the relationship of Christ to men and women. The story of Cardiana and Aliso may seem like window dressing, but structurally it is similar to *The Emancipated Slave of Love* in that the author began his work as a combination allegory-treatise and then abruptly shifted to the sentimental "Story of Two Lovers," with its magic transformations and tales of heroism for love. Like *The Emancipated Slave of Love* also, there is an exaltation of both man and woman, for although the advocate of woman's superiority is a woman, the tragic but faithful Cardiana, nonetheless, it is the author himself, Juan Rodríguez, who brings Aliso to life by using the waters of the fountain. Ultimately, then, it is Juan Rodríguez who is "chosen" to alleviate the suffering of a faithful lover and thus he returns to his favorite role of redeemer of the courtly love movement.

II Cadira del honor (The Seat of Honor)

The companion piece to *The Triumph of Women* is *The Seat of Honor*, Juan Rodríguez's treatise on nobility. The historical reason for the sudden effulgence of works on the origins of nobility and the definition of true nobility was twofold: the polemic of the late Middle Ages initiated by the famous legal canonist, Bartolus of Sassoferrato, and the emergence of a new class of nobility which received its honors for services granted, services which were financial, scholarly, or bureaucratic rather than military. As Anna T. Sheedy has written, "[Bartolus] . . . had a personal interest in the subject, for he belonged to that newer noble class which owed its status not to the possession of feudal estates, but to the special favor of a Prince or to an office which conferred noble rank upon the incumbent."[6] Unlike other countries of Europe, however, the Spanish nobility of the early fifteenth century still furnished important military service to the Castilian crown, for there was still the hated Moor in the south. Thus many members of the traditional nobility who were soldiers or whose estates were conferred upon them for military prowess, such as Juan Rodríguez, quickly came to despise the new class of courtiers and minority members such as converted Jews, whom they felt did not merit either the title or the trappings of nobility.

If Bartolus is the spokesman of the newer, emerging nobility, then Juan Rodríguez is the spokesman of the conservative viewpoint, the traditional beliefs about nobility and its kinship with chivalry, landed property, and high birth. The issue that Juan

Rodríguez seeks to resolve is whether true nobility is the result of virtue and good deeds alone (as Bartolous had argued) or whether lineage is the determining factor. As we shall see, Juan Rodríguez opts for the latter and seeks to justify it on the basis of traditional, classical sources as well as his own reasoning.

The work begins as the author attempts to resolve the dilemma of the young men at the court of John II who are seeking the answer to the question of what constitutes true nobility. In order to arrive at his answer, Juan Rodríguez begins once more with an allegorical setting, claiming that the "seat of honor" is to be found in the "garden of merit," and is wrought of "two fruit-bearing plants, virtue and nobility," and few in his age occupy it although many covet it, for there is also a "seat of false honor" wrought of "two savage plants, fiction and fortune." The author begins by refuting Bartolus, who claimed that riches contribute to magnanimity, which according to both Aristotle and St. Thomas, is a virtue.[7] According to Juan Rodríguez, Bartolus identified the meaning of nobility as generosity, but Juan Rodríguez identifies the meaning with ancestry: "So it is the same to consider that squirarchy (*fidalguia*), gentility, nobility, and generosity differ little; although the insignious civil doctor [Bartolus] says that since generosity . . . is nobility combined with virtue, it is more than just nobility." Juan Rodríguez's basis for equating nobility with ancestry is St. Isidore's ninth book of his *Etymologies*.

Then Juan Rodríguez proceeds, as did Bartolus, to describe the various types of nobility—theological, moral, political, and vulgar—although his major concern, as was Bartolus's, is political nobility, the conferring of a title and privileges by a sovereign or feudal lord. It is Juan Rodríguez's conclusion that the virtuous, if they are basely born, are merely that—virtuous but not noble—although the nobly born may also be virtuous: ". . . it is to be noted that virtue by itself is never nobility, although nobility is sometimes virtue. Thus if the nobility rules virtuously they may truly occupy the seat of honor but even if the ignobly born rule virtuously, they still do not possess nobility and by extension have no right to occupy the seat of honor." Juan Rodríguez's arguments are derived from Aristotle's *Ethics* and the second part of the second book of Aquinas, the latter stating that nobility is not true virtue but a sign of virtue. The final argument is that some nobles may not even be virtuous, but even these are seen to occupy "...the lowest rung on the ladder by which one arrives at the high seat of honor."

The requirements for true nobility are as follows: authority granted by the prince or the crown, purity of lineage, good customs, and ancient wealth. Thus the author states that "...he is not noble who does not possess clear lineage; and consequently, he will not be a true noble, nor will be those who are descended from him, until the fourth generation be purged of the obscurity of the blood line by forgetfulness and that by long possession of good deeds [customs] and ancient wealth."

What incenses Juan Rodríguez is that the sovereign has conferred titles and honors upon so many that are unworthy that they "occupy the seat of false honor" and cause confusion in the kingdom. These are the men who have received the orders of knighthood in the private chambers of the princes without ever having worn armor. Thus he complains further, in complete disagreement with Bartolus, that this new class should not have the right to wear an insignia or claim coats of arms, nor should cities be allowed to display the noble colors—silver and gold—in their heraldry.

The differences between the treatises of Bartolus and Juan Rodríguez are due, in part, to social differences between the two writers. Bartolus was a jurist who received his title for legal and scholarly services rendered to the crown, and sought to justify the position of this new class (akin to the middle class) by the proper use of wealth and diligent service to a prince who needed it partly as a defense against the older, more prestigious nobility. Juan Rodríguez, on the other hand, resented the new nobility precisely because the monarchy was placing more confidence in them to the detriment of the traditional, landed aristocracy. The principal casualties of this policy were members of the poorer, rural nobility, whose younger sons, like himself, were forced to make their living at court, and who took out their hostilities against the *converso* class which they felt was displacing them in favor.

The early fifteenth century in Spain, the era preceding the coming to power of the Catholic kings, was not merely a preimperial, pre-Renaissance and premessianic age, it was also a preinquisitional period with spokesmen like Juan Rodríguez who argued for a return to the old order. Although *The Seat of Honor* was meant to be a tribute to the queen, and therefor in some measure a piece of flattery, it also stresses an aspect of Juan Rodríguez's thoughts which is always present in his works—his concern for the purity of his lineage, in order to be considered a rightful messiah of courtly love in the rest of his literary production, but, more importantly, in this work at least, to be considered an "Old Christian" and therefore not a Jew.

III Bursario o Las Epístolas de Ovidio
(Pocket Novel or The Epistles of Ovid)

The *Pocket Novel* is a translation of Ovid's *Heroides*, in which great liberties are taken with the text. Not only are some of the passages either freely or erroneously translated, but, in addition, there are certain alterations made in accordance with late medieval Spanish taste. For example, the letter from Sappho to Phaon is omitted, presumably because of the rather explicit mention of the lesbian loves of the female protagonist, and preceding each epistle is a rubric in which the author either lauds the classical figures for their "licit love" or reprehends them for their "illicit [that is, adulterous] love." A typical example of this kind of Christian moralizing is the author's rubric before the epistle from Phaedra to Hippolytus: "In order to understand the following letter, one must know that Phaedra was the daughter of King Minos of Crete and the wife of Theseus, king of the Athenians, and she it was who loved Hippolytus, her stepson, who was the son of Theseus and Hippolyta, queen of the Amazons; and he chastely scorned her; and to induce him to love her, she sent him this letter, in which her intention is to beg Hippolytus to love her. The author's intention is to reprehend her for her illicit love." Because of this attitude, certain figures such as Penelope and Hermione are praised for their loyalty and virtue, while others, such as Helen and Medea, are condemned.

Juan Rodríguez appears to have chosen this work for translation because it was a sentimental recasting of epics of classical antiquity. And since most of the letters are written by women who narrate their own heroism and berate their men for disloyalty or perfidy, it is possible that the work was intended for some important woman in the court, perhaps Queen María herself. Most important of all, three epistles, which do not even appear in Ovid's original—the letter from Madreselva to Manseol and the exchange between Troylos and Breçayda—have as their central figures women rather than men.

The "Letter from Madreselva to Manseol" is not so much an epistle as a sentimental novel in miniature, for the work bears considerable resemblance to the third section of *The Emancipated Slave of Love*, "The Story of Two Lovers." The entire epistle occupies only seven pages in Antonio Paz y Melia's edition of Juan Rodríguez's complete works, but a good deal of plot is packed in. Madreselva, the female protagonist, is writing to her lover, Manseol, from prison. It happens that Madreselva is the queen of Caledonia (Scotland), who finds herself ". . . disinherited from [her] throne by the cruel hand of her uncle Aritedio, the brother of Hercules, [her] deceased father. . . ." The queen is in prison specifically because of the treachery of her mother, Adelfa, who claimed that Madreselva's lover, Manseol, had attempted to violate her daughter, and thus caused her daughter to be imprisoned and Manseol brought to the public square for execution. In the midst of her desperation, Creta, Madreselva's servant arrives to tell her that just as Manseol was about to be killed, Artamisa, Madreselva's rival, appeared, claiming that Manseol had attempted to violate her also, but that rather than ask for his head, Artamisa was willing to marry him to avenge her honor. As Adelfa clamored for his death and Artamisa for his hand, and authorities decided in favor of the latter. Artamisa and Manseol supposedly went off to Acaya, leaving Adelfa outraged and Madreselva heartbroken, powerless to avenge herself. After hearing the news, the latter writes to Manseol, begging him to forsake Artamisa, whom she terms an *encantadora* ("sorceress"), and return to the woman whom he truly loves.

It is apparent that there are many similarities between this tale and "The Story of Two Lovers," even though the protagonist this time is female. Ardanlier's death and Madreselva's imprisonment are both the result of evil parents; both are incapable of attaining their thrones, Madreselva because of her usurping uncle and Ardanlier because of his vengeful father; both are of royal blood and both suffer for their loyalty to their respective beloveds. Another point of similarity in the two stories is the element of the supernatural. Ardanlier's death and the subsequent enchantment of his tomb by the efforts of the Princess Yrena bring about the coming of the heroic Macías, from whom Juan Rodríguez claims to be descended. Madreselva not only claims to be a "granddaughter of Jove," but also to have been born in the forest after Hercules slew the lion and fell in love with the nymph Adelfa. Thus her father was a semimortal who became a god, and her grandfather, Jove himself. We could almost expect that had the epistle continued, Juan Rodríguez would have shown himself to be a direct descendant also of Madreselva, unless he was reserving that honor for someone else. Plotting against Madreselva is evil personified, in the figure of Artamisa, a sorceress descended from yet another sorceress, the wicked Çirça.

The fact that Madreselva claims to be a disinherited queen of Scotland recalls the famous "Law of Scotland," which appears in another famous fifteenth-century sentimental novel, Juan de Flores's *Grisel e Mirabella*.[8] In this work, the king of Scotland catches his daughter, Mirabella, with her lover, Grisel, but discovers that according to the "Law of Scotland," one of the lovers must be declared guiltier than the other, and the guiltier of the two, that is the one who initiated the love, is to be burned at the stake, while the other is to be banished. In his work, Juan de Flores has two advocates appear to argue the respective cases for man and woman, as to who is the guiltier party in any love relationship. The two speakers turn out to be none other than the infamous woman hater, Torrellas,[9] and Breçayda,[10] ill-fated lover of Achilles. After the arguments are presented, it is decided that woman is guiltier and that Mirabella should be burned and Grisel banished. However, another element is introduced: the two lovers vie with each other for the honor of being sacrificed, the so-called "combat of generosity,"[11] for neither wishes the other to be declared guilty and burned, and neither could live without the other in perpetual exile. In Juan

de Flores's novel, the solution occurs when Grisel throws himself
into the fire that was prepared for Mirabella, and then she also
plunges into the flames. Thus do the two lovers achieve the
ultimate in sacrifice for love.

The "Law of Scotland," made famous by Juan de Flores,
appears to be an important, implicit element of Juan Rodríguez's
epistle. Manseol is condemned to death as the guiltier party,
and Madreselva is allowed to live, albeit in prison. Also, the
judges, swayed by Artamisa's arguments, allow Manseol to live
in exile, although it may be assumed that the possibility of
death at the hands of her wicked uncle awaits the imprisoned
Madreselva unless Manseol comes to rescue her. The story of
the damsel in distress, typical of the romances of chivalry and
the sentimental novels, is the realistic and psychological pivot
of the story of Madreselva and Manseol. However, the blood
relationship of the characters to figures of classical mythology
elevates the story to the level of the mythic and supernatural—
the mark of Juan Rodríguez—which we must now explore.

The relationship of Artamisa to Manseol recalls that of
Artemis to Hippolytus. Artemis, or Diana, was one of the
sinister goddesses of three forms,[12] and Hippolytus scorned the
love of Phaedra to worship only Artemis. Phaedra's death ultimately led to revenge by the combined forces of Aphrodite and
Poseidon, who brought about the death of Hippolytus. Later,
it is told, Hippolytus was made immortal, and came to be wor-
shipped in Italy under the name of Virbius.[13] The relationship
of Madreselva and the usurping of her throne by her uncle
Aritedio (also called Cadateo in the epistle) recalls the relationship of Hercules to his half brother Iphicles, for Hercules as a
baby killed the two serpents which entered his cradle, while
his half-brother ran away in fear. Thus Madreselva is pure and
courageous, while her half brother is cunning and unscrupulous.

The picture that emerges from the relationship of Madreselva
to Manseol, Artamisa to Manseol, and Madreselva to Aritedio
is that Madreselva is descended from the gods and that Manseol
appears to be the counterpart of Hippolytus who was descended
from a hero, Theseus, and the Amazon, Hippolyta. Interfering
with their love is the sorceress Artamisa, descended from another
sorceress, Çirça, who is presumably Circe, who turned Odysseus's

men into swine. Thus, like *The Emancipated Slave of Love*, the sentimental epistle is an attempt to combine the worlds of classical mythology and the romances of chivalry. Madreselva is the standard damsel of royal blood, but she is also descended from a god. Interfering with their love is an enchantress of the Morgan le Fay–Circe type.

The final two epistles of the *The Pocket Novel* are an interchange between Troylos and Breçayda. In the first letter, Troylos accuses Breçayda of forgetting him and transferring her affections to Diomedes, a sworn enemy of Troy. Readers familiar with Chaucer's *Troilus and Cresseida* and Shakespeare's *Troilus and Cressida* will remember the disrepute into which Cressida or Briseis had fallen as a result of going off with Diomedes and forsaking the noble Troilus.[14] In Juan Rodríguez's work, however, Breçayda defends herself by taking the offensive. As she ends her letter, she relates two allegorical dreams. In the first, she describes herself enclosed by a large rock into which descend an emperor, his empress, and a host of princes, knights, and ladies, all dressed for battle, but apparently in need of repose. As they enter, a knight appears, also dressed for battle, who exhorts his followers to fight and take the rock from the five knights who were holding it, as well as the ensign bearing the banner. As an added detail, the knight who did the exhorting is handed his armor by an old dame. During the second night of dreaming, the meaning of the first dream is explained. The rock is the "rock of true love" (*bien amar*), the emperor and empress are Cupid and Venus, respectively, and the lord of the rock is Vulcan, father of Cupid. The rock symbolizes the firmness of the lover's will. The bold knight who attacked the rock was Troylos himself, and the old dame who handed him the lance was forgetfulness. The other old woman who gave him the banner was disloyalty, while the ensign taken prisoner after the battle was his loyal heart, and the five knights defending the rock, his five senses. Thus the dream is an allegory to show that Troylos is both forgetful and disloyal to her as a lover, for he has doubted that she is still in love with him. The letter ends with Breçayda lamenting her misfortune and begging Troylos to be victorious over the Greeks and recapture her.

For the modern reader, the *Pocket Novel*'s interest resides almost exclusively in the epistle of Madreselva to Manseol, because it is a sentimental novel in miniature or, perhaps, the beginning of a sentimental novel left unfinished. The story of Madreselva represents a further attempt by the author to elevate the status of the faithful courtly lover, male or female, to that of a god, an attempt which succeeded admirably in the third part of *The Emancipated Slave of Love*, "The Story of Two Lovers." The epistle is less successful artistically for two reasons: it is too short, and once more, as in the second part of *The Emancipated Slave of Love*, "Solitary and Dolorous Contemplation," the attempt to intertwine a chivalric tale with elements drawn from classical mythology is a bit strained. Only the female protagonist's name, Madreselva, "Forest-Mother," recalls the element of enchantment, whereby the tombs of the lovers were transformed magically in *The Emancipated Servant*. Perhaps Madreselva's birth in the forest, after the killing of the presumably "Thespian" lion by her father, Hercules, endows her with special powers which are heroic if not magical. In any event, Juan Rodríguez has produced another interesting literary experiment, which succeeds in fascinating and tantalizing the reader without fully satisfying.

IV *Conclusion*

Fifteenth-century prose, like poetry of the same era, was in an experimental stage and produced mixed results. New genres like the sentimental novel were attempted; treatises on secular topics in vogue were written in the vernacular rather than in Latin and revealed at once the boldness of the authors and the limitations placed upon them structurally and conceptually by Scholasticism. Crude attempts were made to display erudition, often by merely listing names from antiquity without really alluding to actual content. Juan Rodríguez himself, for instance, lists Homer, Seneca, Ovid, Plato, Terence, Juvenal, Horace, Cicero, Dante, Quintilian, and several others as influences on his style in the first part of *The Emancipated Slave of Love*. The indiscriminateness of this list shows that the classical learning which we call humanism, the study of original texts of classical antiquity without modifications by ecclesiastical authority, was, for Spaniards like Juan Rodríguez, virtually unknown in the early fifteenth century. Dissatisfaction with, or loss of confidence in, papal authority was evidently stimulating interest in those classical works which commented upon the secular issues of the day, such as courtly love, true nobility, and the rights of women, but a purely empirical approach, that is, a reliance on one's experience alone without mention of the "Authorities," would have been unthinkable for the Spaniard of the early fifteenth century.

Within the narrow confines set up by Scholasticism's approach to topical issues, the prose writer was forced to write a formal treatise, following the rules of medieval rhetoric, perhaps including a bit of allegory, as Juan Rodríguez was prone to do, and then resolve the question in a manner consonant with existing orthodoxy. This is the method followed by Juan Rodríguez in both his poetry and prose, but it is more evident in his prose treatises than elsewhere. In *The Triumph of Women*, for example, a list of fifty reasons, most of them drawn from respectable sources, back up the author's "liberal" contention that woman is superior. And another host of arguments, based on Aristotle and Aquinas for the most part, support the author's "conservative" opinion in *The Seat of Honor* that the only true nobility is the traditional one based on lineage, landed property, and military service performed for the suzerain.

The Emancipated Slave of Love, which was originally intended to be a treatise also, presents far more complex problems than does either of his two prose treatises or the *The Pocket Novel*. First, Juan Rodríguez's work does not conform to the other types of sentimental novel, such as the works of Boccaccio, Aeneas Sylvius's *Historia de doubus amantibus* (*The Story of Two Lovers*), Diego de San Pedro's *Cárcel de amor* (*The Prison of Love*), or Juan de Flores's two works, *Grisel e Mirabella* and *Grimalde e Gradissa*. Juan Rodríguez's work does not deal with an adulterous relationship as do the works of the Italians, nor is its structure epistolary but rather heterogeneous, with the third and most significant part being an interpolated novel with many strange, supernatural elements drawn from the romances of chivalry. It has been said that the sentimental novel's primary focus is the analysis of the effects of love and the dangers inherent in the love relationship, be it adulterous or merely rebellious, as in the case of Juan Rodríguez's "Story of Two Lovers." However, it appears that Juan Rodríguez's main focus in *The Emancipated Slave of Love* is not an exaltation of woman nor of love, but rather the exaltation of self, that is, his own apotheosis. This kind of thinking, which, as we have discussed previously, is prevalent throughout his poetry, like a variation on a theme, reaches its culmination in his prose, where the author is free to invent a long, chivalric tale to legitimize his claims of being the one and only true messiah of love, whose birth is prefigured by the lives of Ardanlier and Macías.

It is in line with our thinking that the second part of *The Emancipated Slave of Love*, "Solitary and Dolorous Contemplation," should be an artistic failure, for the classical erudition displayed in this section reveals the undigested nature of ancient thought and mythology, whereas the author's evident assimilation of the spirit and technique of the romances of chivalry show his medieval orientation, despite an obvious dissatisfaction with medieval institutions. Indeed, the entire work is a tortured and at times tortuous criticism of courtly love and the court. Unable to cope with court intrigue or his social disadvantage, the author finds himself in a lover's purgatory which offers him no escape until he evokes the tale of Ardanlier and Liessa, which eventually leads to the visit by Synderesis who, presumably, will guide him to a lover's paradise.

A variation on the same theme is the amorous "Epistle from Madreselva to Manseol," likewise a fragment, although the protagonist is now female and a composite drawn from scattered elements of classical mythology. For that very reason, the work is less convincing, for Madreselva traces her lineage to Jove and Hercules rather than to any chivalric figure. The entire *Pocket Novel* is itself a good example of undigested erudition, for the epistles do not appear in their pure Ovidian form, but rather preceded by an epigraph praising or condemning the licit or illicit love affair described. And the Spanish psyche was seemingly not prepared for the details of the female loves of Sappho.

Juan Rodríguez should and probably will be best remembered as the author of *The Emancipated Slave of Love*, but he does show a great deal of originality, if not technical mastery, in his other prose works. Insofar as men were capable of rebelling within the constraints of the Church, noble or royal patronage, and the literary norms of the age, Juan Rodríguez was a rebel with at least two specific causes: equality in the love relationship and the acquisition of eternal fame.

CHAPTER 8

Conclusion

IN the previous pages we have attempted to present the life and works of Juan Rodríguez de la Cámara, a literary figure virtually unknown to readers who are not specialists in medieval or Renaissance Spanish literature. It has been our contention that Juan Rodríguez's life and works are relevant for today's reader because of his concern for the equality of men and women in the love relationship and because of his questioning of authority.

His concern for equality of the sexes and his questioning of authority may be traced in part to his era, a time of transition, upheaval, and civil wars. The Spanish king, John II, was, as we have seen, a patron of the arts and reigned over a court where poetry flourished, but was unfortunately a weak monarch, whose favorite, Alvaro de Luna, ruled by default and incurred the wrath of powerful upper nobility in his quest for power. In the Church, the Great Schism was coming to a close, but matters were not really resolved until the threat to Papal supremacy from the Conciliar movement eventually faded away. During this era, also, women were attacked in verse by Pedro Torrellas and in prose by the archpriest of Talavera, but when Queen María, wife of John II, sought defenders, many were to be found.[1]

In this transitional climate, we have attempted to define and distinguish the literary movement which came originally from France—courtly love. It has been our contention that courtly love had been seriously modified since its early days in the south of France and that it arrived with certain suppositions repugnant to the Spaniard, principal among them the superiority of the lady and the subservience of the troubadour, a situation evolving historically from their respective social roles.

Juan Rodríguez's significance is that he constitutes the principal spokesman for what was to become the dominant Spanish attitude toward courtly love—the complete inability to accept an inferior position. In poem after poem, culminating in his novel, *The Emancipated Slave of Love,* Juan Rodríguez prepares careful and, at times, legalistic arguments, for his authority to question the lady's presumed superiority. This authority to question such a basic premise is predicated on the assumption that courtly love was itself a kind of parallel or rival religion to Christianity, and that in order to have any kind of authority, authority must be claimed by various means: the authority of revelation, such as in "The Ten Commandments of Love"; the authority of self-imposed canonization, such as in "The Seven Joys of Love," or by the authority of enchantment, such as occurs in *The Emancipated Slave of Love.*

Juan Rodríguez will in all likelihood be best remembered for his prose, and especially because he is the creator of Spain's first sentimental novel. In *The Emancipated Slave of Love,* the interpolated section entitled "The Story of Two Lovers," is a culmination of all his previous attempts at tearing down the elaborate structure of courtly love and replacing it with a more realistic conception of love. As Juan Rodríguez establishes the genre, love becomes a form of rebellion against repressive parents and oppressive social mores, and this rebellion can only end tragically in death. In Juan Rodríguez's tale, Liessa's murder and Ardanlier's suicide are symbolic of the fate of those who would defy authority and flee the stultifying atmosphere of the royal courts. The Princess Yrena's inability to win Ardanlier's love, and her shrine to the two lovers represents courtly love's yielding to the natural forces of love removed from the artificialities of the court.

The conversion of the lover's tomb into a kind of Holy Grail of courtly love, to be attained only by the greatest of courtly lovers, Macías, represents another culmination in Juan Rodríguez's works, the final establishment of a courtly love "lineage," whereby he, Juan Rodríguez, seeks to identify himself as a descendant of that figure who supposedly suffered physical death for love. For Juan Rodríguez, banishment from the court of Castile was an equivalent martyrdom which established his courtly love credentials.

Despite the significance of *The Emancipated Slave of Love,* it should not be forgotten that Juan Rodríguez authored one of the most ingenious defenses of women ever written in Spain, *The Triumph of Women.* Few writers of his day would have claimed that women were superior to men, and it is to Juan Rodríguez's credit that he used the traditional Scholastic authorities—Aristotle, the Bible, and the Church fathers—to argue for what was then an unpopular cause.

Finally, Juan Rodríguez was always a defender of his homeland, Galicia, even though it had already been absorbed by Castile and was rapidly becoming castilianized. By making his homeland the center of the courtly love universe in "The Story of Two Lovers," Juan Rodríguez returned to days when Santiago de Compostela competed with Rome as the holiest shrine in all of Christendom.

For the professional literary critic the early fifteenth century presents many problems. It seems often that writers of this period were like painters attempting to depict a landscape with an ill-equipped palette. The writers of that era had to contend with a vernacular language still evolving, with old forms, such as allegory and Scholasticism, frankly declining, while new forms, such as humanism, were as yet imperfectly assimilated or even understood.

In politics, the Spaniards were aching to expel the Moors, demand religious conformity,[2] unify the Peninsula, and to unify their own country and to stop the civil wars. Much of this expectation seemed to express itself as a need for a messianic figure under whose leadership the Spaniards would attain greatness. Such greatness was finally attained a century later.

It was Juan Rodríguez who seemed to sense this need of his countrymen. He chose as his vehicle of expression courtly love literature rather than politics or religion, but the same pattern was present. He declared himself to his fellow nobles and courtiers to be the true messiah of love—the one who would lead the faithful out of bondage and into the Promised Land. It was he who by his "death" would redeem the masses of the faithful. Few, we suppose, took this bravado seriously, but his

York: The Hispanic Society of America, 1920), III, 47–50, for Caxton's translation from the *Codex Calistas,* Book 3, "The Journey of St. James' Body."

14. Since Lupa means "wolf" in Provençal, we are almost tempted to believe that Juan Rodríguez may have wished to recall the relationship of Queen Lupa to St. James as being reminiscent of the Provençal troubadour Peire Vidal, who dressed himself in wolf-skins and had himself hunted by his lady's dogs in order to show that he was in love with a lady named "Lupa." For a fuller version of this tale, see Francesco Novati, "Un avventura di Peire Vidal," *Romania* 21 (1892), 78–81.

15. For A. Castro's view of the cult of Santiago as a needed warrior Patron Saint to counteract the effects of Mohammed, see his *La realidad histórica de España* (México: Porrúa, 1966), pp. 326–57.

16. *Ibid.,* p. 330.

17. See Roger Sherman Loomis, *The Grail, From Celtic Myth to Christian Romance* (New York: Columbia University Press, 1964), p. 250, and by the same author, *Celtic Myth and Arthurian Romance* (New York: Columbia University Press, 1927), p. 193.

18. See Castro, p. 330.

19. See Roger S. Loomis, *Celtic Myth and Arthurian Romance* (New York: Columbia University Press, 1927), pp. 191–93.

20. Dinko Cvitanovič, *La novela sentimental española* (Madrid: Editorial prensa española, 1973), p. 90.

21. For a modernized edition of *Amadís de Gaula,* see *Amadís de Gaula,* Edición refundida y modernizada por Angel Rosenblat (Buenos Aires: Lozada, 1940).

Chapter Seven

1. See A. Paz y Melia, ed., *Obras de Juan Rodríguez de la Cámara (o del Padrón)* (Madrid: Ginesta, 1884), p. xxix.

2. For a discussion of Pero Torrellas and the controversy he awakened, see Barbara Matulka, *The Novels of Juan de Flores and Their European Diffusion. A Study in Comparative Literature* (New York: Institute of French Studies, 1931), pp. 111–37.

3. See *Alfonso Martínez de Toledo, Arcipreste de Talavera o Corbacho. Edición, introducción y notas por J. González Muela* (Madrid: Clásicos Castilia, 1970), p. 17.

4. Giovanni Boccaccio, *De claris mulieribus,* available in translation as *Forty-Six Lives,* trans. Henry Parker, Lord Morley, and ed. Herbert G. Wright (London: Published for the English Text Society by H. Milford, Oxford University Press, 1943).

thoughts merely parodied the political and religious hopes of the succeeding generations.

Juan Rodríguez should rightfully take his place as a skillful writer of courtly love poetry—as a master of ecclesiastical parody, casuistry, and striking verbal imagery. He should also be remembered as the champion of equality of the sexes in love and as defender of Galicia—a minority nation seeking to preserve its cultural heritage.

We hope that the readers of this series will discover that the early fifteenth century contains many interesting figures in literature and politics, not the least of which is a minor noble from Padrón in Galicia—Juan Rodríguez de la Cámara.

Notes and References

Chapter One

1. In fact, entire poems by Juan Rodríguez were used by other poets to make larger works. Such a poem was known as a *glosa*.

2. *Grisel e Mirabella* and *Grimalte e Gradissa*. For a discussion of these works, see Barbara Matulka, *The Novels of Juan de Flores and Their European Diffusion* (New York: Institute of French Studies, 1931).

3. P. Fidel Fita and Aureliano Fernández Guerra. *Recuerdos de un viaje a Santiago de Galicia* (Madrid: Lezcano, 1880), p. 35.

4. Gonzalo Argote de Molina. *Nobleza de Andalucía* (Jaén: Muñoz Garnica, 1866), pp. 693–94.

5. See María Rosa Lida de Malkiel, "Juan Rodríguez del Padrón: vida y obras," *Nueva revista de filología hispánica* 6 (1952), 326.

6. Antonio Paz y Melia, *Obras de Juan Rodríguez de la Cámara (o del Padrón)* (Madrid: Ginesta, 1884), p. 45.

7. Ibid., pp. 174–75.

8. P. Atanasio López, *Nuevos estudios crítico-históricos acerca de Galicia* (Madrid: CSIC, Instituto Padre Sarmiento de Estudios Gallegos, 1949), I, 274.

9. "O desuelada, sandia," in Paz y Melia, pp. 29–30.

10. López, "El franciscanismo en España durante los pontificados de Eugenio IV y Nicolás V a la luz de los documentos vaticanos," *Archivo Iberoamericano* 25 (April–June, 1932), 222–23.

11. Pedro José Pidal, "Vida del trovador Juan Rodríguez del Padrón," *Revista de Madrid* (November, 1839), pp. 15–31.

12. According Pidal, ibid., p. 31n., the queen was probably Marie d'Anjou, wife of Charles VII of France.

13. See Pidal, *Cancionero de Baena*, (Madrid: Rivadeneyra, 1851), p. 696.

14. For an account of the life of Macías, see Hugo Rennert, *Macias O Namorado, A Galician Trobador* (Philadelphia: privately published, 1900); Kenneth H. Vanderford, "Macías in Legend and Literature," *Modern Philology* 31 (1933–34), 35–63, and H. Tracy Sturken, Macios O Namorado: Comment on the Man as Symbol," *Hispaia* 44 (1951), 47–51.

15. See Rennert, p. 3.

16. The editor of the only critical edition of Juan Rodríguez's complete works, Antonio Paz y Melia, states that the *Crónica gallega de Iria* had been attributed to Juan Rodríguez, but that the evidence was against it. See Paz y Melia, pp. xxxii–xxxiv. For the decline of Galician as a literary language in the fifteenth century, see José Filgueira Valverde, "Lírica medieval gallega y portuguesa," in Guillermo Díaz-Plaja, *Historia general de las literaturas hispánicas* (Barcelona: Editorial Barna, 1949), I, 612–13.

17. For a negative judgment of Macías's poetry, see Lida de Malkiel, p. 326.

18. See María Rosa Lida de Malkiel, *Juan de Mena, Poeta del prerrenacimiento español* (México: Fondo de cultura económica, 1950), in which she attempts to depict Juan de Mena as a true forerunner of Renaissance culture in Spain.

19. Three different historical perspectives on the early fifteenth century may be seen in the following: Roger Bigelow Merriman, *The Rise of the Spanish Empire in the Old World and in the New*, Vol. 1, *The Middle Ages* (New York: Macmillan, 1918); Américo Castro, *La Realidad histórica de España*, 3rd ed. (México: Porrúa, 1966); and Robert B. Tate, *Ensayos sobre la historiografía peninsular del siglo XV*, trans. de Jesús Díaz (Madrid: Gredos, 1970). Merriman's work shows the Spaniards preparing their political and military structure for Empire; Castro shows how many *conversos*, such as Juan Alfonso de Baena, sought to ". . . incite King John II of Castile to loftier undertakings, a characteristic need of the converted Jews in the fifteenth century" (p. 63) and Tate shows the role of *converso* historians writing in both Latin and the vernacular urging imperial undertakings.

20. Although John II technically assumed the throne in 1406, his uncle, the powerful Ferdinand of Antequera, later to become Ferdinand I of Aragon, was appointed regent until he died in 1416, and was succeeded by his son Alfonso V of Aragon who held the regency until John II became of age in 1419.

21. For the life of John II's favorite, who virtually ruled Castile until he fell into disgrace and was beheaded, see *La Crónica de Don Alvaro de Luna, Edición y estudio por José María Carriazo* (Madrid: Espasa-Calpe, 1940).

22. John Huizinga, *The Waning of the Middle Ages. A Study of the Forms of Life, Thought and Art in France and the Netherlands in the XIVth and XVth Centuries*, trans. F. Hopman (Garden City, N.Y.: Doubleday, 1954).

23. Raymond Lincoln Kilgour, *The Decline of Chivalry as Shown in the French Literature of the Late Middle Ages* (Cambridge, Mass.: Harvard University Press, 1937).

24. See Castro, pp. 48, 63.

25. See Friedrich Heer, *The Medieval World. Europe 1100–1350*, trans. Janet Sondheimer (New York: The New American Library, 1963), "Jews and Women," pp. 309–23.

26. For an analysis of Rojas's attitude toward courtly love in *La Celestina*, see María Rosa Lida Malkiel, *La originalidad artística de La Celestina* (Buenos Aires: Eudeba, 1962), pp. 215–20.

27. The parody of courtly love in Cervantes should more correctly be termed a parody of chivalresque love, such as was found in the romances of chivalry. See Chapter 2 of this study.

28. For a discussion of the "debarbarization" of the Castilian court, see Théodore Joseph Bodet (Comte de Puymaigre), *La cour littéraire de Don Juan II* (Paris: Franck, 1873).

29. For a possible influence of nominalism on the poetry of the early fifteenth century, see Enrique Morena Báez, "El gótico nominalista y las 'coplas' de Jorge Manrique," *Revista de filología española* 53 (1970) 95–113.

30. *El Victorial. Crónica de Don Pero Niño, Conde de Buelna por su alférez Gutierre Diez de Games. Edición y estudio por Juan de Mata Carriazo* (Madrid: Espasa-Calpe, 1940).

Chapter Two

1. For a discussion of *Fin'Amors*, see A. J. Denomy, *"Fin'Amors*: The Pure Love of the Troubadours: Its Amorality and Possible Source," *Mediaeval Studies* 7 (1945), 139–207, especially 174–76; and René Nelli, *L'Érotique des troubadours* (Toulouse: Privat, 1963), pp. 132–39.

2. Nelli, pp. 24ff.

3. Ibid., p. 36.

4. Moshé Lazar, *Amour Courtois et "Fin'Amors" dans la littérature du XIIe siècle* (Paris: Librairie Klincksieck, 1964).

5. Nelli, p. 25.

6. Nevertheless, the Arabs of Spain, such as Ibn Hazm, were influenced by the so-called "love of Baghdad" or *Udri*, in which desire was intensified by practicing a bizarre kind of chastity which permitted touching the beloved but did not allow sexual fulfillment. See A. R. Nykl's English translation of Ibn Hazm's treatise, *A Book Containing the Risala Known as the Dove's Neck-Ring about Love and Lovers* (Paris: Librairie Orientaliste Paul Guethner, 1931).

7. See Nelli, pp. 41–53 for a discussion of Neoplatonic Arabic eroticism. For a discussion of the possible influence of Avicenna, see Denomy, "An Inquiry into the Origins of Courtly Love," *Mediaeval Studies* 6 (1944), 247–55.

8. See Nelli, pp. 105–56, "L'Érotique de 1150."

9. See Friedrich Heer, *The Medieval World. Europe 1100–1350*, trans. by Janet Sondheimer (New York: The New American Library, 1963), pp. 157–96.

10. This midpoint between wholly physical and wholly spiritual love is well described by Denomy's discussion of the Provençal term *jois* ("joy"): "Love of a woman of worth keeps the lover in a state of joy. That permanent condition of bliss is the lover's natural abode. . . ." "*Jois* Among the Early Troubadours: Its Meaning and Possible Source," *Mediaeval Studies* 13 (1951), 179.

11. The term "mixed love" in which love is consummated even though the lover continues to serve his lady as a vassal is viewed differently by different authors. According to Andreas Capellanus, mixed love (*mixtus amor*) quickly puts an end to desire. See John Jay Parry's translation of Andreas Capellanus's *De amori libri tres*, *The Art of Courtly Love* (New York: Ungar, 1964), p. 164. However, Nelli, pp. 191–92, claims that mixed love does little or no harm to the essence of the courtly love relationship once the male has shown his sincerity by his abstention and his suffering, and the female herself may wish the love to be consummated also, either out of desire or out of a sense of compassion; that is, wanting to grant "clemency."

12. For a discussion of *trobar clus*, see Alfred Jeanroy, *La poésie lyrique des troubadours* (Toulouse: Privat, 1934), II, 34–35.

13. For a discussion of this anonymous writer and his four stages of love, see Camille Chabaneau, *Deux mss. provençeaux du xive siècle* (Paris, 1888), p. 149.

14. According to Nelli, pp. 159 and 181n., the earliest meaning of *drut* for the Provençal troubadours was the lady's physical lover, usually a member of the upper nobility, rather than the lady's *fin aman* or "true lover" in a spiritual sense.

15. Nelli, pp. 63–65.

16. For a discussion of Andreas Capellanus and the Condemnation of 1277, see Denomy, "The *De Amore* of Andreas Capellanus and the Condemnation of 1277," *Mediaeval Studies* 8 (1946) 107–49; Douglas Kelly, "Courtly Love in Perspective: The Hierarchy of Love in Andreas Capellanus," *Traditio* 24 (1968) 119–47, and Nelli, pp. 247–63.

17. See Nelli, pp. 264–328, "L'École de Toulouse."

18. For a discussion of this so-called "school," see Henry R. Lang, *Cancioneiro gallego-castelhano. The Extant Galician Poems of the Gallego-Castilian Lyric School (1350–1450)* (New York: Charles Scribner's Sons, 1902), pp. xi–xvi.

19. In one of the poems found in *Siervo libre de amor*, "Cerca el alba, quando estan," the final three stanzas end with quotes from Macías's "Catyvo de mi tristura," as found in Paz y Melia, ed., *Obras de Juan Rodríguez de la Cámara (o del Padrón)* (Madrid: Ginesta, 1884), p. 79.

20. See Lang, pp. 161, 165, 167, 168, 186, 234.

21. See José Filgueira Valverde, "Lírica medieval gallega y portuguesa," in *Historia general de las literaturas hispánicas,* ed. Guillermo Díaz-Plaja (Barcelona: Editorial Barna, 1949), I, 612–13.

22. Ibid. See also Ramón Menéndez Pidal, *Poesía árabe y poesía europea* (Buenos Aires: Espasa-Calpe, 1943), pp. 62–63.

23. Lida de Malkiel, "La hipérbole sagrada en la poesía castellana del siglo XV," *Revista de filología hispánica* 8 (1946), 129.

24. Ibid., p. 30.

25. For a discussion of the relationship between the Scholastic treatise and its manifestation in the arts, see Erwin Panofsky, *Gothic Architecture and Scholasticism* (Cleveland: Meridian, 1964).

26. See Nelli, p. 184: "For them [the Provençal troubadours], love constituted a sort of class revindication, an aspiration towards equality, on the only plane in which it could at that time be obtained: that of sentiment."

27. Maurice Valency, *In Praise of Love. An Introduction to the Love-Poetry of the Renaissance* (New York: Macmillan, 1958), p. 151, describes the process of falling in love as follows: "... the troubadours were agreed that love was in the first place a lesion of the eye. It was born of light, of an image which, after penetrating the eye, descended to the heart and lodged there, kindling desire."

28. Lazar, p. 117.

29. Ibid., p. 112.

30. Ibid., p. 114.

31. See Nelli, p. 294.

32. Ibid., p. 72.

33. See Helen Flanders Dunbar, *Symbolism in Mediaeval Thought and Its Consummation in the Divine Comedy* (New York: Russel and Russel, 1961), p. 58.

34. Denomy, *"Fin'Amors"* p. 167 (see note 1).

35. Scattered throughout the stanzas of a Provençal poem, we

find code words known as *senhals* ("signs"), such as *bon vezi* ("good neighbor") or *midons* ("my lord") which stood for the lady's name.

36. See Lang, p. 234.

37. See Nelli, pp. 116–17.

38. The *pie quebrado* is the half line of four syllables. See Dorothy Clotelle Clarke, "A Chronological Sketch of Castilian Versification Together with a List of Metric Terms," *University of California Publications in Modern Philology* 34, no. 3 (1952), pp. 285–87.

39. This is an emendation. The original reads "y virtud mayor de *si.*"

40. The first of the Provençal troubadours, Guillaume IX, Duke of Poitiers, in his later poetry chose to submit to his lady and consider her his superior, even though he remained proud and aristocratic. See Nelli, p. 92.

41. For a discussion of the lover's need for self-control despite his ardor, see Otis H. Green, "Courtly Love in the Spanish *cancioneros,*" *Proceedings of the Modern Language Association* 64 (1949), 267.

42. See Nelli, pp. 199–209.

43. M. C. D'Arcy, *The Mind and Heart of Love. Lion and Unicorn. A Study in Eros and Agape* (Cleveland: Meridian, 1956), p. 352, defines *Caritas* as being "God's special love and man's response to it as inspirited and energized by it."

44. Antonio Paz y Melia, p. 400.

45. For Juan Rodríguez's impact on fifteenth-century literature, see Lida de Malkiel, "Juan Rodríguez del Padrón: influencia," *Nueva revista de filología hispánica* 8 (1954), 1–38.

46. W. Y. Evans Wentz, *The Fairy Faith in Celtic Countries* (Oxford: Oxford University Press, 1911), p. 227, states the following: ". . . ancient and modern Celts have likewise regarded themselves as incarnations and reincarnations of ancestors and fairy beings."

Chapter Three

1. See Otis H. Green, "Courtly Love in the Spanish *cancioneros.*" *Proceedings of the Modern Language Association* 64 (1949), 267.

2. See Maurice Valency, *In Praise of Love. An Introduction to the Love-Poetry of the Renaissance* (New York: Macmillan, 1958), pp. 157–59, and A. J. Denomy, "*Jois* Among the Early Troubadors: Its Meaning and Possible Source." *Mediaeval Studies* 13 (1951), 179.

3. Valency, p. 178.

4. A similar allusion to the women of Seville is made by the late fourteenth- and early fifteenth-century *converso* poet, Alfonso Alvarez de Villasandino in the *Cancionero de Baena,* ed. de José María de Azáceta (Madrid: CSIC, 1966), nos. 28–31, 67–76.

5. Robert B. Tate, *Ensayos sobre la historiografía peninsular del siglo XV,* versión española de Jesús Díaz (Madrid: Gredos, 1970), p. 16.

6. For a description of Regulus's deed, see Sir Paul Harvey, The Oxford Companion to Classical Literature (Oxford: The Clarendon Press, 1940), p. 35.

7. See Suero de Ribera, "La ley que fizo Suero de Ribera que tales deuen ser los que dessean ser amados," and Hernando de Ludueña, "Dotrinal de gentileza que hizo el comendador Herhando de Ludueña, maestresala de la reyna nuestra señora . . . ," both found in Ramón Foulché Delbosc, *Cancionero castellano de siglo XV* (Madrid: Bailly-Bailliere, 1912–1915), II, 191–92 and 718–34 respectively.

8. The ballads are the outstanding example.

Chapter Four

1. See Richard Bernheimer, *Wild Men in the Middle Ages. A Study in Art, Sentiment and Demonology* (Cambridge, Mass.: Harvard University Press, 1952).

2. See Francisco Paula de Fernández de Córdoba, "Sobre el lobo y su presencia en Galicia," *Cuadernos de Estudios Gallegos* 18, Fascicle 54 (1963), 92–118.

3. *Macbeth,* act 2, sc. 2, lines 61–63.

4. In the *Cancionero de Baena,* "Biue leda si podras" is preceded by the following epigraph, no doubt the work of a scribe: "Juan Rodríguez del Padrón composed this song when he became a friar in Jerusalem after taking leave of his lady."

5. See Karl Vossler, *La poesía de la soledad en España* (Buenos Aires: Losada, 1946), p. 12.

6. See Henry R. Lang, *Cancioneiro gallego-castelhano. The Extant Galician Poems of the Gallego-Castilian Lyric School (1350–1450)* (New York: Charles Scribner's Sons, 1902), pp. xi–xvi.

7. See René Nelli, *L'Érotique des troubadours* (Toulouse: Privat, 1963), p. 262.

8. See Sara Sturm, "The Presentation of the Virgin in the *Cantigas de Santa Maria,*" *Philological Quarterly* 49 (1970), 1–7.

9. For a discussion of the possible chronology of Rodríguez's prose, see Paz y Melia, ed., *Obras de Juan Rodríguez de la Cámara (o del Padrón)* (Madrid: Ginesta, 1884), pp. xxi–xxii.

10. For a discussion of Rodrigo Cota, see Richard F. Glenn, "Rodrigo Cota's 'Dialogo entre el Amor y un Viejo': Debate or Drama?" *Hispania* 48 (1965), 51–56.

11. For a discussion of the awakening Renaissance sensibility in *Siervo libre de amor,* see Edward J. Dudley, "Structure and Meaning in the Novel of Juan Rodríguez: *Siervo Libre de Amor,*" (Ph.D. dissertation, University of Minnesota 1963; available from University Microfilms, Ann Arbor), pp. 29, 109–10.

12. Alessandra Bartolini, "Il canzoniere castigliano de San Martino delle Scale (Palermo)," *Boletín del Centro di Studi Filologici e Linguistici Siciliani* 4 (1956), 147–87.

13. Charles H. Leighton, "Sobre El planto de Pantasilea," *Hispanófila,* no. 10 (September, 1960), 9–14.

14. Eugenio de Ochoa, *Catálogo razonado de los manuscritos españoles existentes en la biblioteca real de Paris* (Paris: Imprenta Real, 1844), p. 487. Ochoa was the first to attribute the work to the Marqués de Santillana, and later he had the concurrence of both José Amador de los Ríos, *Obras de don Iñigo López de Mendoza, Marqués de Santillana* (Madrid: J. Rodríguez, 1852), pp. 410–17, and Marcelino Menéndez y Pelayo, *Antología de poetas líricos castellanos* (Madrid: Hernando, 1890–1908), V, cviii–cxix.

15. According to Ochoa, p. 487, in no manuscript is the work ever really attributed to the Marqués.

16. See Paz y Melia, pp. 18–19.

17. See Howard R. Patch, *The Goddess Fortuna in Mediaeval Literature* (Cambridge, Mass.: Harvard University Press, 1927), for the historical development of Fortune from Roman literature to the medieval era.

Chapter Five

1. David W. Foster, *The Early Spanish Ballad* (New York: Twayne, 1971), pp. 13–45.

2. With the exception of perhaps the Marqués de Santillana, who said the following: "Of the lowest order ("ínfimos") are those who without any order, rule or care compose those ballads and songs which the people of base and servile condition enjoy."

3. For a discussion of the formulistic diction, see Ruth House Webber, "Formulistic Diction in the Spanish Ballads," *University of California Publications in Modern Philology* 34, no. 2 (1951), 175–278.

4. Manuscript number is add. no. 10431.

5. Hugo Rennert, "Der spanische Cancionero des British Mus.

[British Museum Additional MS. 10431]," *Romanische Forschungen* 10 (1895), 1–176.

6. Rennert, "Lieder des Juan Rodriguez del Padron," *Zietschrift für romanische Philologie* 17 (1893), 557.

7. Menéndez y Pelayo, *Orígenes de la novela* (Madrid: NBAE, 1905), I, cclxxxvii.

8. Paz y Melia, ed., *Obras de Juan Rodríguez de la Cámara (o del Padrón)* (Madrid: Ginesta, 1884) p. 56.

9. See Francisco Caravaca, "El Romance del Conde Arnaldos en el Cancionero manuscrito de Londres," *La Torre* 62 (1968), 77.

10. Manéndez Pidal, *Romancero hispánico* (Madrid: Espasa-Calpe, 1953), I, 260.

11. Ibid., pp. 64–65.

12. For a discussion of the relationship of the Flying Dutchman theme to Conde Arnaldos, see Leo Spitzer, "The Folkloristic Pre-Stage of the Spanish Romance 'Conde Arnaldos,'" *Hispanic Review* 23 (1955), 173–87.

13. See John T. Reid, "St. John's Day in Spanish Literature," *Hispania* 18 (1935), 401–12.

14. For ballad chronology, see S. Griswold Morley, "The Chronological List of Early Spanish Ballads," *Hispanic Review* 13 (1945), 273–87.

15. Pidal, later reprinted in the *Cancionero de Baena* (Madrid: Rivadeneyra, 1851), pp. 689–95.

16. See Azáceta, "El pequeño cancionero," in *Estudios dedicados a Menéndez Pidal* (Madrid: CSIC, 1957), vol. VII, part 1, pp 83–111.

17. Only the first stanza composed of eight lines is found.

18. See Rennert, "Lieder," pp. 544–58.

19. *The Divine Comedy of Dante Alighieri.* Trans. and comment by John D. Sinclair (New York: Oxford University Press), I, "Inferno," pp. 78, 11. 121–23.

20. Three possible readings for the seventh line, third stanza are "otro," "otros," and "otra."

21. See Lida de Malkiel, "Juan Rodríguez del Padrón: influencia," *Nueva revista de filología hispánica* 8 (1954), 10n.

22. María Rosa Lida de Malkiel, *Juan de Mena, poeta del prerrenacimiento español* (México: El Colegio de México, 1950).

23. For a view of mannerism as a cyclical phenomenon, see Ernst Robert Curtius, *European Literature and the Latin Middle Ages*, trans. Williar R. Trask (New York: Harper & Row, 1963), and Wylie Sypher, *Four Stages of Renaissance Style. Transformations in Art and Literature 1400–1700* (Garden City, N. Y.: Doubleday, 1955).

Chapter Six

1. See Anna Krause, "El 'tractado novelístico de Diego de San Pedro," *Bulletin Hispanique* 54 (1952), 253 for the expansion and development of the Scholastic treatise in fifteenth-century Spain.

2. See Dudley, pp. 6–7.

3. See Robert H. Tate, *Ensayos sobre la historiografía peninsular del siglo XV*, trans. Jesús Díaz (Madrid: Gredos, 1970), p. 280.

4. See Dudley, "Structure," p. 34. Another observation by Dudley is that the autobiographical nature of *Siervo libre de amor* is similar in many respects to *The Dove's Neck-Ring* of Ibn Hazm.

5. According to Tate, p. 17, Hercules was a very significant figure for Spanish historiographers of the Middle Ages, for through Hercules the Spaniards established a mythology of their national origin in the manner of Aeneas's supposed founding of Rome. According to the historian Rodrigo Ximénez de Rada, Archbishop of Toledo, Hercules traveled to Spain and there passed the reins of government of the three provinces of Galicia, Lusitania (Portugal), and Bética (Andalusia) to his companion Hispano, the eventual founder of Spain.

6. See John T. Reid, "St. John's Day in Spanish Literature," *Hispania* 18 (1935), 401–12.

7. According to Dudley, "Court and Country: The Fusion of Two Images of Love in Juan Rodríguez's *El Siervo Libre de Amor*," *Proceedings of the Modern Language Association* 82 (1967), 119, structural shifts in the sentimental novel take place as the author's interest moves ". . . the events themselves to the author's subjective reactions."

8. The Spanish preference for the unmarried woman is well known. See Otis H. Green, "Courtly Love in the Spanish *cancioneros*," *Proceedings of the Modern Language Association* 64 (1949), 247–301, esp. p. 283n.

9. Dudley, p. 119, says the following: "The thematic fusion of joy and suffering, of flesh and the spirit, is also expressed in the union of the worlds of nature and of court. Just as the Princess Yrena comes to the forest and is transformed into a vestal, so the courtly world is drawn to the lovers' tomb in a type of chivalric pilgrimage."

10. Ibid.

11. Ibid., p. 118.

12. See Carlos Martínez-Barbeito, *Macías el enamorado y Juan Rodríguez del Padrón*, Biblioteca de Galicia, Vol. 4 (Santiago de Compostela: Sociedad de Bibliófilos Gallegos, 1951), pp. 116–19.

13. See Georgiana Goddard King, *The Way of Saint James* (New

5. See Jacob Ornstein, "La misoginia y el profeminismo en el literatura castellana," *Revista de filología hispánica* 3 (1941), 219–32.

6. Anna T. Sheedy, *Bartolus on Social Conditions in the Fourteenth Century* (New York: Ams Press, 1967), p. 105.

7. In the fourth book of the *Convivio*, Dante claimed that riches could not confer nobility, since wealth in itself is base and brings a burden to the soul. But Sheedy, pp. 117–18, writes that Bartolus rejected this opinion, feeling that wealth could help attain and perpetuate nobility.

8. See Barbara Matulka, *The Novels of Juan de Flores and Their European Diffusion* (New York: Institute of French Studies, 1931), pp. 58–68.

9. For the life and works of Torrellas, see above (Matulka), pp. 99–137.

10. The changing attitude towards Briseis or Breçayda was evident in the fifteenth century according to Matulka, p. 91.

11. Ibid., p. 79.

12. See Robert Graves, *The Greek Myths* (Baltimore: Penguin, 1951), I, 83.

13. Ibid., p. 358.

14. See Matulka, pp. 90–91.

Chapter Eight

1. Barbara Matulka, *The Novels of Juan de Flores and Their European Diffusion* (New York: Institute of French Studies, 1931), pp. 69–70.

2. For a contemporary discussion of the Inquisition, see Henry Kamen, *The Spanish Inquisition* (New York: New American Library, 1968).

Selected Bibliography

PRIMARY SOURCES

1. Prose

Siervo libre de amor is found in two anthologies: Carlos Martínez-Barbeito, *Macías y Juan Rodríguez del Padrón* (Santiago de Compostela: Sociedad de bibliófilos gallegos, Biblioteca de Galicia, Vol. 4, 1951, 153–94), and *Siervo libre de amor. Siete gozos de amor. Diez mandamientos de amor. Canciones* (Buenos Aires: Editorial Nova, 1943).

2. Poetry

There are some selections in the above works as well as in Marcelino Menéndez y Pelayo's *Antología de poetas líricos castellanos* (Madrid: Hernando, 1890–1908), in which Volume 12 contains "Ballads Attributed to Juan Rodríguez del Padrón" (pp. 541–42), and Hugo Rennert's "Lieder des Juan Rodriguez del Padron," *Zeitschrift für romanische Philologie* 17 (1893), 544–58, which contains the ballads and the lengthier version of "Ardan mis dulçes membranças." The following *Cancioneros* or *Songbooks* contain one or more poems attributed to Juan Rodríguez: *Cancionero de Juan Alfonso de Baena*, ed. José María de Azáceta, 3 vols. (Madrid: CSIC, 1966); *Cancionero de Lope de Stúñiga, códice del siglo XV* (Madrid: Rivadeneyra, 1872); *Cancionero de Módena*, Karl Volmöller, "Der Cancionero von Modena," *Revista de filología* 10 (1899), 449–70; *El Cancionero de Palacio*, ed. Francisca Vendrell de Millas (Barcelona: CSIC, 1945); *Cancionero de Roma*, ed. E. Canal Gómez, 2 vol. (Florencia, Sansoni, 1935); *Cancionero general de Hernando del Castillo*, 2 vols. (Madrid: Sociedad de bibliófilos españoles, 1892); *Cancionero musical de los siglos XV y XVI*, ed. Francisco Asenjo y Barbieri (Madrid: Academia de Bellas Artes de San Fernando, 1890); and *Le Chansonnier espagnol d'Herberay des Essarts (xvᵉ siècle)*. Édition précédée d'une étude historique par Charles V. Aubrun (Bordeaux: Féret, 1951).

3. Complete Works

PAZ Y MELIA, ANTONIO. *Obras de Juan Rodríguez de la Cámara (o del Padrón)* (Madrid: Ginesta, 1884). The only extant critical edition of the complete works.

SECONDARY SOURCES

1. Books dealing with Juan Rodríguez's Period

CASTRO, AMERICO. *La realidad histórica de España*. 3rd ed. México: Porrúa, 1966. Also available in translation as *The Structure of Spanish History* (Princeton: Princeton University Press, 1954). An outstanding analysis of medieval Spain, with the early fifteenth century viewed as a period of great turmoil, with the *converso* society, brilliant and insecure, vying with the traditional nobility in all areas, including politics and literature.

DIAZ-PLAJA, GUILLERMO. *Historia general de las literaturas hispánicas*. Vol. 1. Barcelona: Editorial Barna, 1949. Within this volume are studies by individual specialists of the various genres of early fifteenth-century Spanish literature. The most significant article is J. Filgueira Valderde's "Lírica medieval gallega y portuguesa," pp. 545–642, an excellent discussion of the decline of Galician as a literary language.

HEER, FRIEDRICH. *The Medieval World. Europe 1100–1350*. Translated by Janet Sondheimer. New York: New American Library, 1963. One of the best histories of the era immediately preceding the early fifteenth century and indispensable for a proper understanding of Scholasticism and the role of women and Jews.

HUIZINGA, JOHAN. *The Waning of the Middle Ages. A Study of the Forms of Life, Thought and Art in France and the Netherlands in the XIVth and XVth Centuries*. Translated by F. Hopman. Garden City, N. Y.: Doubleday, 1954. A study of the dwindling power of the aristocracy in the fourteenth and fifteenth centuries and its attempt to bolster its diminishing importance by lavish display and pageantry.

LIDA DE MALKIEL, MARIA ROSA. *Juan de Mena, poeta del prerrenacimiento español*. México: Fondo de cultura económica, 1950. This is the first work to consider the early fifteenth century as a "pre-Renaissance," mainly because poets such as Juan de Mena were experimenting with such innovations as humanism, Latinate vocabulary, and Italian verse forms which did not become popular until the latter half of the century.

MENÉNDEZ Y PELAYO, MARCELINO. *Historia de la poesía castellana en la Edad Media*. Vol. 2. Madrid: V. Suárez, 1914. A comprehensive study of fifteenth-century Spanish poets and an introduction to the era by Spain's foremost champion of orthodoxy.

MERRIMAN, ROGER BIGELOW. *The Rise of the Spanish Empire in the Old World and in the New*. Vol. 1. New York: Macmillan,

1918. A traditional historian's account of the Spanish prepara-
tions, both physical and psychological, for their coming empire
in America and Europe, with considerable emphasis upon the
struggle between the aristocracy and the crown as an impeding
factor.

TATE, ROBERT B. *Ensayos sobre la historiografía peninsular del
siglo XV.* Translated by Jesús Díaz. Madrid: Gredos, 1970. A
discussion of several topics treated by medieval Spanish historians. Two of the best chapters deal with the late medieval
views on classical mythology and the role of converted Jews as
imperial propagandists.

2. Books about Juan Rodríguez

LOPEZ, P. ATANASIO. *La literatura crítico-histórica y el trovador
Juan Rodríguez de la Cámara o del Padrón.* Santiago de Compostela: Tipografía de El Eco Franciscano, 1918. Interesting
mainly for biographical data related to Juan Rodríguez's entering the Franciscan Order.

MARTINEZ-BARBEITO, CARLOS. *Macías el enamorado y Juan Rodríguez
del Padrón.* Biblioteca de Galicia, Vol. 4. Santiago de Compostela: Sociedad de bibliófilos gallegos, 1951. Valuable for a
discussion of the life and works of Macías, as it clears up many
of the misstatements made about the relationship of the latter
to Juan Rodríguez. Excellent bibliography.

3. Periodical Articles

DUDLEY, EDWARD J. "Court and Country: The Fusion of Two Images
of Love in Juan Rodríguez's *El Siervo Libre de Amor*." *Proceedings of the Modern Language Association* 82 (1967), 117–20.
Court and country depicted as two distinct and conflicting
environments symbolized by Ardanlier's two loves: Liessa, the
"natural" love of the country (or forest), and the Princess
Yrena, the "stylized" love of the court.

LIDA DE MALKIEL, MARIA ROSA. "Juan Rodríguez del Padrón: vida
y obras." *Nueva revista de filología hispánica,* 6 (1952), 313–58.
A lengthy discussion of Juan Rodríguez's legend and literary
production. The article has an unfortunate tendency to dichoto-
mize the life and works of Juan Rodríguez and Juan de Mena,
claiming that the former represents all that is "reactionary" and
"medieval," while the latter typifies all that is "progressive"
and "Renaissance." Despite this negative factor, the article is

significant because of the author's judgments on the three
chivalric ballads and "O desuelada, sandia."

—————. "Juan Rodríguez del Padrón: influencia." *Nueva revista de
filología hispánica* 8 (1954), 1–38. In many respects, this is a
superior article to the above because of the great amount of
bibliographical information about all of the works, prose and
poetry, influenced by Juan Rodríguez's legend and literary
production.

4. Dissertations

DUDLEY, EDWARD J. "Structure and Meaning in the Novel of Juan
Rodríguez: *Siervo Libre de Amor*." Ph.D. dissertation, Univer-
sity of Minnesota, 1964. Available from University Microfilms,
Ann Arbor. An outstanding thematic and structural study of
Juan Rodríguez's most famous work.

5. Courtly Love Studies

D'ARCY, M. C. *The Mind and Heart of Love, Lion and Unicorn.
A Study in Eros and Agape*. Cleveland: Meridian, 1956. An
orthodox explanation of *Caritas*, or Christian grace, and its
relationship to courtly love.

GREEN, OTIS H. "Courtly Love in the Spanish *cancioneros*." *Proceedings of the Modern Language Association* 64 (1949),
247–301. An erudite study of the themes found in Provençal
courtly love poetry and their manifestation in Castile. Unfortunately, the author claims that courtly love in Spain showed no
marked differences from its Provençal forerunner.

LAZAR, MOSHÉ. *Amour Courtois et "Fin Amors" dans la littérature
du XIIᵉ siècle*. Paris: Librairie Klincksieck, 1964. Courtly love
is viewed as an evolving phenomenon beginning in the twelfth
century in the south of France. In its early stages, courtly love
is a spiritual sensation which derives always from physical love,
and the former does not exist in isolation without the latter.

LE GENTIL, PIERRE. *La poésie lyrique espagnole et portugaise à
la fin du moyen âge*. Vol. 1. Rennes: Plihon, 1949. An erudite
study of the various courtly love themes and their expression
in the Iberian Peninsula. The author feels that there is a
strong northern French (as opposed to Provençal) influence on
Castilian courtly love poetry.

LEWIS, C. S. *The Allegory of Love*. London: Oxford University
Press, 1946. An outstanding contribution to courtly love studies.

Courtly love is viewed as a rival or "truant" from the true religion, Christianity, with the former possessing its own rites, deities, and body of laws.

LIDA DE MALKIEL, MARIA ROSA. "La hipérbole sagrada en la poesía castellana del siglo XV." *Revista de filología hispánica* 8 (1946), 121–30. An outstanding article which clearly demonstrates the peculiar Spanish genius for ecclesiastical parody.

NELLI, RENÉ. *L'Érotique des troubadours.* Toulouse: Privat, 1963. To date, the most significant reevaluation of Provençal courtly love. The author relies heavily on folklore and ethnography, and this makes his work both stimulating and controversial.

6. The Sentimental Novel

CVITANOVIC, DINKO. *La novela sentimental española.* Madrid: Editorial prensa española, 1973. A historical overview of the Spanish sentimental novel beginning with Juan Rodríguez's *The Emancipated Slave of Love.* This work is especially strong in its identification of Renaissance elements in Juan Rodríguez's works, both poetry and prose.

MATULKA, BARBARA. *The Novels of Juan de Flores and Their European Diffusion.* New York: Institute of French Studies, 1931. An extremely erudite and perceptive study of feminism, antifeminism, and chivalric and sentimental conventions and their manifestations in the Spanish sentimental novel and other prose works of the fifteenth century.

7. Folklore and Myth

BERNHEIMER, RICHARD. *Wild Men in the Middle Ages. A Study in Art, Sentiment, and Demonology.* Cambridge, Mass.: Harvard University Press, 1952. An excellent study of the conventions and tensions present in the theme of wild men who willingly submitted to their ladies in such works as the romances of chivalry, courtly love poetry, and even the graphic arts.

LOOMIS, ROGER SHERMAN. *Celtic Myth and Arthurian Romance.* New York: Columbia University Press, 1927. The tracing of the Celtic, pre-Christian myths which were Christianized by such authors as Chrétien de Troyes who molded them into the elements of the romances of chivalry.

————. *The Grail. From Celtic Myth to Christian Symbol.* New York: Columbia University Press, 1964. The pre-Christian basis for the legend of the Holy Grail, the most famous Arthurian quest.

Index

147